# 100

## THINGS TO DO IN
# MINNESOTA
# NORTHWOODS
## BEFORE YOU
# DIE

Itasca State Park
Photo courtesy of Vicki Foss

# 100

## THINGS TO DO IN
# MINNESOTA
# NORTHWOODS
## BEFORE YOU
# DIE

• • • • • • • • • • • • • • • • • • • • • • • •

## JULIE JO LARSON

REEDY PRESS

Library of Congress Control Number: 2020950002

ISBN: 9781681062976

Design by Jill Halpin

Cover photo: Courtesy of Vicki Foss

Printed in the United States of America
21 22 23 24 25    5 4 3 2 1

# DEDICATION

To my family, friends, and all the kind people
I met on my Minnesota Northwoods explorations:
thank you for sharing your wisdom, knowledge,
and love of our region.

Betty's Pies
Photo courtesy of Julie Jo Larson

# CONTENTS

● ● ● ● ● ● ● ● ● ● ● ● ● ● ● ● ● ● ● ● ● ● ● ● ●

• • • • • • • • • • • • • • • • • • • • • • • • • • • • •

● ● ● ● ● ● ● ● ● ● ● ● ● ● ● ● ● ● ● ● ● ● ● ● ● ● ● ●

## Culture and History

• • • • • • • • • • • • • • • • • • • • • • • • • • • •

● ● ● ● ● ● ● ● ● ● ● ● ● ● ● ● ● ● ● ● ● ● ● ● ● ● ● ●

Bear in Tree
Photo courtesy of Vicki Foss

# ACKNOWLEDGMENTS

Thanks to Krista Soukup from the Blue Cottage Agency for putting me in touch with the great team at Reedy Press. I appreciate the opportunity to share my love of the Minnesota Northwoods with all of you. To my family and friends for suggesting "just one more thing" to check out, and to my photographer and co-conspirator Vicki Foss for taking many of the pics of these "things" thank you. MsStorians Yvonne Doust and Leigh Melby, you have patience beyond measure and always go the extra mile.

I owe deep gratitude to my mom, Patricia Hood, and my Momma Larson (Peggy) for being great mentors. Thanks to my husband, Stephen, and children, Alex, Sorina, Morgan, and their soulmates for being my cheerleaders and to Maria, Joe, Nancy, CLC, TRIO, and the entire Larson family for encouraging me to wander at will. I would also like to acknowledge some of the positive effects of COVID-19, such as pushing my patience and creativity, and helping me appreciate the little things in life, like traveling safely during a pandemic and sleeping in my own bed.

# PREFACE

In the fall of 2010, I embarked on a wild and wonderful adventure that changed the trajectory of my life and my career. I returned to college after a two-decade break and in the process developed a deep sense of wanderlust. Wanderlust? Yes, wanderlust as in the strong desire to wander, travel, and explore the world beyond one's backyard.

Wandering is fine on one's own. However, I find it much more enjoyable with my motley crew of women called the MsStorians. Together we traverse the Minnesota Northwoods in search of history, fun, and flavorful beverages. Our adventures are legendary and regularly appear in regional magazines as "MsStorian Adventures."

The book you are holding (thank you for purchasing a copy) contains snippets of our MsStorian Adventures. It's our way of sharing some cool things with you and hopefully our stories will encourage you to wander a bit. You might consider buying a new pair of mukluks, we covered a lot of ground for this book... in all kinds of weather.

For my contribution to Reedy Press's *100 Things* series, I strayed a bit from the formula and chose to broaden my scope from one city to a larger region. This is the "Land of 10,000 Lakes," four seasons, and uncharted wilderness. Hardy people live in the Minnesota Northwoods year-round, and less hardy people vacation here in the summer. (Let's face it, not everyone enjoys five months of winter.)

To help you traverse in style, we've included a few suggested itineraries and lists of seasonal activities at the end of this book. So, grab your copy of *100 Things to Do in Minnesota Northwoods Before You Die*, and get a move on. Adventure awaits!

—Julie Jo Larson, LSW

Lewis the Husky at the Roundhouse Brewery
Photo courtesy of Vicki Foss

# FOOD AND DRINK

# TASTE POOR GARY'S
## CHICKEN WILD RICE PIZZA

Poor Gary's Pizza in downtown Moose Lake is a family-owned mom-and-pop joint where small-town atmosphere meets big-time pizza taste. Minnesota Northwoods's favorite grain, wild rice, partners with tender chicken, real mozzarella cheese, and a creamy alfredo sauce on top of a thin, crispy crust. Wild rice adds a hearty texture and smoky flavor to this local favorite. The taste sensation is so popular, Poor Gary's added wild rice pizza to their frozen take-home menu, so you can enjoy it back at the cabin. Many tourists say this is their favorite pizza stop between the Twin Cities and Duluth. I concur.

Not a pizza lover? Poor Gary's offers sub sandwiches, hot soup, and fresh salads.

Poor Gary's Pizza, 401 Elm Ave., Moose Lake
(218) 485-8020

# TIP

Take in an afternoon matinee at Lake Theatre (#31) before grabbing a Poor Gary's chicken wild rice pizza to go. Eat your pizza on the patio at the Moose Lake Brewery (#5).

# ENJOY A MS. GALENA
## AT THE ROUNDHOUSE BREWERY

Ms. Galena was one of the Brainerd Lakes Area's "businesswomen" in the late 1800s. She was a hardworking gal who believed in getting things done, even if life went a bit sour at times. The Roundhouse Brewery in Nisswa offers Ms. Galena sours in a variety of seasonal fruit flavors. This kettle-soured beer is made with dark cherry puree and real fruit flavors. It's perfect after a hot day on the lake or bike trail. Not a fan of sour beers? Roundhouse Brewery has a variety of craft beers and nonalcoholic beverages.

The Roundhouse Brewery moved from Brainerd to their new location in 2020. In addition to a large taproom, Roundhouse has an entertainment facility, large outdoor seating area, and a stage for live music. The outdoor area is dog-friendly, and there's plenty of room for kids to run.

Roundhouse Brewery, 23836 Smiley Rd., Nisswa
(218) 963-BREW, info@roundhousebrew.com

# FILL UP WITH A PASTY
## FROM PASTIES PLUS

Pasties Plus owner, Ruth Wepsala Pedley, compares a pasty to a calzone on steroids. Since 1997, each pasty is handmade according to Ruth's grandmother's special recipe. The pasties are stuffed with meat and root vegetables such as rutabaga, potatoes, and carrots. Five filling varieties are offered daily on the menu. The German pasty is a fall favorite with sauerkraut, thinly sliced bratwurst, onion, and diced potatoes.

Pasty Plus's seating is very limited, but no worries. The log shape of a pasty makes it an easy meal to eat on the go—perfect for picnics by the river. Don't forget to order gravy for dipping. Pasties freeze well and reheat easily at home. Pre-ordering is recommended to reduce wait time.

Pasties Plus, 1405 NW 4th St., Grand Rapids
(218) 398-2994, pastiesplus.com

# TRY JAMS AND JELLIES
## AT BUTKIEWICZ FAMILY FARM

Established in 1904, the Butkiewicz Family Farm near Kettle River supplies area communities with jams, jellies, fresh produce, lamb, and beef products. Pick up a few jars of raspberry jam or pepper jelly for a breakfast treat. You can conveniently order online and have them delivered right to your door. Holistic Wellness Services in downtown Moose Lake also stocks a great variety of Butkiewicz jams and jellies. They are located at 499 Arrowhead Lane, in the heart of the downtown.

Stop by the farm in December to start a new family tradition. Cut down a Christmas tree and then drive through the farm's holiday light display. Your children will be nestled in their beds with the vision of pine needles and fresh jam dancing in their heads.

Butkiewicz Family Farm, 6710 Butkiewicz Rd., Kettle River
(218) 273-6100, butkiewiczfamilyfarm.com

# ENJOY THE VIEW
## AT MOOSE LAKE BREWERY

The craft beer craze reaches across much of the Minnesota Northwoods—there are breweries galore. Even so, few can compete with Moose Lake Brewery's beautiful view. Try their Whiskey Chip Stout while watching the fall sun reflect over Moosehead Lake. This stout is brewed with hazelnut and Madagascar Bourbon and packs a punch. At 12 percent ABV, it's a great beer to sip outside with friends while enjoying a Poor Gary's Pizza (#1). When the last rays of daylight fade away, venture into the taproom for some small-town hospitality.

Moose Lake Brewery's giftshop offers glassware and clothing with their fun logo on it. Their shirts are super soft and comfortable and are perfect for a bike ride on the beautiful Willard Munger Trail. It's just across the street from the Brewery!

Moose Lake Brewery, 244 Lakeshore Dr., Moose Lake
(218) 485-4585, mooselakebrewing.com

# SATISFY YOUR SWEET TOOTH
## AT FANCY PANTS CHOCOLATES

Quality chocolate is always in season at Fancy Pants Chocolates in downtown Brainerd. Chocolatier Nancy Williams opened her doors in the summer of 2002 with a modest menu. Her repertoire has grown to over three dozen varieties of chocolates. Many are offered with either fine milk chocolate from Belgium or dark chocolate from Colombia.

Even the most discriminating chocoholic can't resist melt-in-your-mouth Bailey's Truffles, chewy caramel squares, or Cashew Bear Claws. Williams keeps a variety of lovely boxes and baskets to hold your chocolate treasures, perfect for special occasions. Stock changes daily, so pre-ordering your favorites for the holidays is encouraged.

Fancy Pants Chocolates, 704 Laurel St., Brainerd
(218) 828-7844, fancypantschocolates.com

# FIND BACON AND MORE
## AT THIELEN MEATS

Since 1922, four generations of Thielens have smoked lean, delicious Northwoods bacon to perfection over sweet maple chips. Can you smell that goodness? No wonder people drive hours to buy a pound, or ten, or twenty. (Did I mention their volume discounts?)

But bacon isn't the only meat you'll find at Thielen Meats in Pierz. They're a full-service meat market specializing in just about every fresh and smoked meat you can think of. No wonder folks voted Thielen Meats the best butcher shop in Minnesota!

They also offer all the fixings: seasonal vegetables, crackers, breads, BBQ sauce, and more. Grab a handful of jerkies for the ride home. Your tastebuds will thank you.

Thielen Meats, 310 N Main St., Pierz
(320) 468-6616, thielen-meats.com

---

### TIP

Bring a cooler of ice to keep your meats fresh and cold when traveling through the Northwoods. You'll want to make sure there's plenty of room to stock your home freezer.

---

# PRIORITIZE DESSERT
## AT BETTY'S PIES

Go ahead—devour dessert before your meal. It's a Northshore tradition at Betty's Pies. The legacy began in 1956 when Betty's father, Aleck Lessard, opened a fish shack near Two Harbors. Betty baked desserts to sweeten things up. Her baked goods soon overtook the fish shack. In 1958, the fish shack was replaced by Betty's Café. Soon Betty was making 100 pies daily, with hand-rolled lard, flour, and love-filled crusts.

Today, owners Carl Ehlenz and Marti Sieber offer pies made from many of Betty's time-tested recipes. Pies are offered in three varieties: cream, baked, or crunch-topped. I highly recommend their Five Layer Chocolate or Dutch Apple pies. Betty's Pies offers pre-orders so your favorite pies are ready when you arrive. A take-out menu full of picnic lunch favorites will give your family something hearty to eat on the way to the cabin or resort.

Betty's Pies, 1633 Highway 61, Two Harbors
(877) 269-7494, bettyspies.com

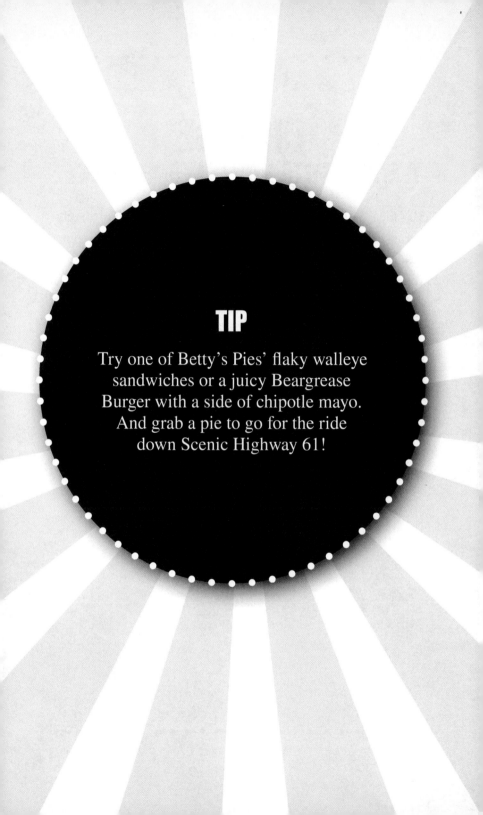

## TIP

Try one of Betty's Pies' flaky walleye sandwiches or a juicy Beargrease Burger with a side of chipotle mayo. And grab a pie to go for the ride down Scenic Highway 61!

# CHOOSE
## A MINNESOTA NORTHWOODS WINE

Let's face it, when you think of Minnesota Northwoods beverages, local wine doesn't usually come to mind—but it should! Minnesota wineries offer great-tasting wine varieties with added fun such as wine tours, art demonstrations, date nights, and so much more.

Traveling north of Duluth to see fall colors? Try North Shore Winery's Boundary Waters Red Wine. Visiting Alexandria for a fishing weekend? Carlos Creek Winery is known for live music and their Ruby Minnescato. Hiking near Bemidji? Try a bottle of Black Currant Wine at Forestedge Winery in Laporte. Celebrating a special occasion with friends in the Brainerd Lakes Area? Stop at Dennis Drummond Wine Company for their award-winning Rosé, and enjoy a meal at their bistro.

**Northshore Winery**
202 Ski Hill Rd., Lutsen
(218) 481-9280, northshorewinery.us

**Carlos Creek Winery**
6693 County Rd. 34 NW, Alexandria
320-846-5443, carloscreekwinery.com

**Forestedge Winery**
35295 MN-64, Laporte
(218) 224-3535, forestedgewinery.com

**Dennis Drummond Wine Company**
11919 Thiesse Rd., Brainerd
(218) 454-3392, ddwco.com

For more Minnesota wineries,
go to www.minnesotagrown.com.

# BIKE
## TO BITES GRILL & BAR

Located on the Paul Bunyan Trail (#54) in Pine River, Bites Grill & Bar is the perfect pit stop when you're on an excursion. Pull up your bike and enjoy two spacious outdoor patios surrounded by mature trees and wildflowers. There is ample green space for your little ones to stretch their legs or play on the game patio. You'll see small-town living up close and experience the natural lure of the Northwoods.

If you need to get out of the sun for a bit, Bites has plenty of room indoors, too. Marvel at the beautiful pine log structure while enjoying daily specials which include lobster-stuffed walleye, Cajun seafood pasta, and unicorn cheesecake. Stop on a Sunday morning for Bites's fresh brunch and a Best of the Lakes Bloody Mary. Bites is known for their made-from-scratch meals and friendly, small-town service.

Bites Grill and Bar, 2793 State Hwy 371 SW
(218) 587-2564, bitesgrill.com

# ENJOY
# PREMIUM ICE CREAM
## AT VICTUAL

Victual is located in Crosby, a small mining town which was voted one of the "Smartest and Best Places to Live" by *Outhouse Magazine* in 2018. A year later, Victual owners embraced their motto, "Northern living, improved," by offering super premium ice cream, artisanal farmstead cheeses, specialty liqueurs, and more. Victual serves instant brain freezes with their never-from-mix ice cream, or you can take your favorite flavor to go in pint or quart containers. While you're there, stock up on their fancy crackers, cured meats, and hard-to-find cheeses. It's not what you'd expect in the Northwoods! Bikers, hikers, paddlers, and couch potatoes have discovered refueling is easy with a stop at Victual.

Victual, 124 W Main St., Crosby
(218) 545-1000, shopvictual.com

### TIP
Grab an assortment of cheeses and crackers before venturing over to Cuyuna Brewing Company (#16).

# TRY POUTINE WITH YOUR BEER
## AT FITGER'S BREWHOUSE
## BREWERY AND GRILLE

Fitger's Brewhouse is Duluth's oldest brewery and the area's oldest taproom. How old is it, you ask? It's so old, the building is on the National Register of Historic Buildings. Visitors and townsfolk have been wetting their whistle on the shores of Lake Superior with Fitger's beer since 1857. Beer is still the number-one reason most stop at Fitger's Brewhouse, but a close second is their grille. The grille offers classics like burgers and local favorites.

Enter poutine, a staple of Canada, our neighbor to the north. Add French fries topped with white cheese curds, jalapenos, and bacon all slathered in Brewhouse beer gravy. And, what beer goes best with poutine? I recommend the Starfire Pale Ale with a shot of Apricot.

Fitger's Brewhouse Brewery and Grille, 600 E Superior St., Duluth
(218) 279-2739, fitgersbrewhouse.com

# TIP

Take a self-guided tour, and explore
every corner of the complex. Don't
forget to see the Bob Dylan exhibit (#30).
Maps are located in the museum and
throughout Fitger's. When you're
done, fill a growler for home.

# EAT WITH UNREGISTERED GUESTS

## AT THE PALMER HOUSE HOTEL, RESTAURANT, AND PUB

Kelley Freeze puts her guests into two categories: registered and unregistered. The difference? The registered guests pay for their meals and the unregistered don't, because they are no longer living. The Palmer House Hotel, Restaurant, and Pub is included on the "Most Haunted in Minnesota" list. KARE 11 TV, *Minnesota Monthly*, and even *TripAdvisor* rank the Palmer House as a top spot for paranormal activity. The Palmer is also a top-notch place to eat.

For lunch, I prefer the Hawaiian chicken salad with Palmer's homemade poppy seed dressing. I encourage you to start your dinner with a seasonal chicken wild rice salad followed by a hand-cut ribeye. Ask the bar manager for the evening drink specials. Be moderate and don't blink, or the dapper fellow by the bar might disappear as quickly as your sweet potato fries.

The Palmer House Hotel, Restaurant, and Pub,
500 Sinclair Lewis Ave., Sauk Centre
(320) 351-9100, thepalmerhousehotel.com

## TIP

If meeting an unregistered guest sounds like fun to you, sign up for one of Kelley's after-hours tours.

# ENJOY A MILKSHAKE
## AT GORDY'S HI-HAT

There are milkshakes, and then there are Gordy's Hi-Hat milkshakes. Gordy's shakes are so good, they were featured on the Food Network's *Diners, Drive-Ins, & Dives* with Guy Fieri. Fieri's favorite shake? Fresh, real blackberry with rich, creamy vanilla ice cream. In all, Gordy's has almost a dozen other varieties on the menu, or you can mix multiple flavors together for a taste all your own. Add an order of hand-battered onion rings and a hand-patted cheeseburger for the full drive-in effect.

For over 50 years, Gordy and Marilyn Lundquist's family has offered old-fashioned carhop service from early spring until late summer. A milkshake at Gordy's Hi-Hat in Cloquet is worth the trip.

Gordy's Hi-Hat, 415 Sunnyside Dr., Cloquet
(218) 879-6125, gordys-hihat.com

# TASTE THAI
## AT UDOM'S THAI RESTAURANT

Udom's Thai Restaurant is ranked number one in Hackensack, and many customers claim it's the best Thai food in Minnesota. But don't take their word for it. Try the Pad Thai for yourself! Menu items vary in spice level, but all are cooked to order with authentic ingredients. If you love Thai food, try Udom's on your next trip up north.

Udom's Thai Restaurant, 106 State St., Hackensack
(218) 675-5513

### TIP
Visiting in the winter? Udom's is open Wednesday through Saturday, but get there early . . . doors close at 7 p.m.

# RELAX
## AT CUYUNA BREWING COMPANY

Cuyuna Iron Range runs through Crosby and neighboring communities. The name "Cuyuna" was formed by combining prospector Cuyler Adams's first name with his trusty dog's, Una. Cuyler and Una loved their community, as do the locals today. After a hard day biking on a red dirt trail or boating in a deep, clear blue mine pit, relax with a Range-made beer and genuine Range hospitality. Beer at Cuyuna Brewing Company pays tribute to Cuyuna's 80-year mining past with names like Manhigh Stout, Ranger Strong Pale Ale, and Hair Force One.

Stop by the Cuyuna Brewing Company to visit with friends, play a board game, and enjoy a cold beverage. The beer list sheds light on local history, and the servers can tell you even more about the Cuyuna experience.

Cuyuna Brewing Company, 1 E Main St., Crosby
(218) 866-0914, cuyunabrewing.com

# GET BREAKFAST
## AT DULUTH GRILL

Forget the big chain restaurants. If you're an "all-day" breakfast lover, you'll love Duluth Grill. It's conveniently located in west Duluth, near Lake Superior Zoo and downtown shopping. This locally owned diner serves everything from classic American comfort food to contemporary dishes and desserts. And did I mention they have all-day breakfast?

A local favorite is the "Chicken and Whaaaaat?" It's an unusual combination of breakfast flavors on one plate—buttermilk-fried chicken and a house-made pancake with bacon and corn, topped with spicy maple-coffee-bacon syrup, and sprinkled with goat cheese and scallions. Chicken and Whaaaaat? is a seriously good way to refuel before hitting the Lake Superior Harbor. Duluth Grill is a popular diner, so add your name to the waitlist online just before your visit.

Duluth Grill, 118 S 27th Ave. W, Duluth
(218) 726-1150, duluthgrill.com

# EAT LUTEFISK
## AT A LUTHERAN CHURCH

Minnesota Northwoods is home for many Scandinavians, a hearty culture that thrives on food from both land and water. One of their most noted dishes is lutefisk. Lutefisk is a Lutheran church Christmas tradition, along with Lefse. Most people have tried Lefse, but what is lutefisk?

Church ladies and men spend over a week carefully soaking whitefish in rotations of cold water and lye. Once cooked and salted, lutefisk becomes semi-translucent and gelatinous. It's one of those foods you try once, just to say you did. Or, you try it and love it. There is no in-between with lutefisk. To find a Lutheran church serving lutefisk, check the local newspapers in December, or ask the locals when you're out and about. Questioning if lutefisk is for you? Take heart, meatballs are often paired during these suppers. Even picky eaters love meatballs.

### TIP
Old, Lutheran churches are well preserved in the Northwoods. Their stained-glass windows glow at dusk and dawn. Try to arrive early enough to watch the sun set through these one-hundred-year-old treasures.

# PICK UP FARM-FRESH PRODUCE AND MORE
## AT FARMERS MARKETS

From early spring to late fall, farmers markets offer fresh produce, honey, jelly, spices, jerky, crafts, and more. Each market operates on different days of the week, so if you don't find that perfect tomato on Tuesday, try the neighboring town on Wednesday.

The Minnesota Department of Agriculture and statewide producers partnered up to create Minnesota Grown. In addition to a comprehensive website, Minnesota Grown publishes a free catalog listing farmers markets, farms, wineries, breweries, apple orchards, pumpkin patches, and tree farms in each region.

A typical Northwoods growing season ends in late September. But Butkiewicz Family Farms (#4) and other growers have extended their growing season by up to a month. Their secret? Heated high tunnel greenhouses! Juicy, fresh tomatoes were available at the Moose Lake and Hinckley Farmer Markets well into October 2020. Sounds delicious to me!

Minnesota Grown, www.minnesotagrown.com

# SAVOR BROWN SUGAR TROUT
## AT RUSS KENDALL'S SMOKEHOUSE

A trip up the Northshore is not complete without a stop at the oldest fish smokehouse on Scenic Drive. Since the early 1900s, Russ Kendall's Smokehouse has produced meaty and delightfully woodsy smoked fish. Their secret lies in using fish supplied daily by Lake Superior fishermen. Two favorites are the brown sugar trout and the smoked whitefish. Kendall's also sells a variety of crackers, fish spreads, jerky, and smoked cheeses. I love the cheese curds.

Here's the secret to a great smoked fish experience at Kendall's: Bring a few paper plates and a fork with you. Next, buy a box of crackers with your fish, and head through the door on the left. It will lead to an old bar area which has plenty of space for families to picnic on rainy days. The wall posters tell the story of early Lake Superior fishing.

Russ Kendall's Smokehouse, 149 Scenic Dr., Knife River
(218) 834-5995, russellkendall.com

# STEP INTO YESTERYEAR
## AT LAST TURN SALOON AND EATERY

Step into Last Turn Saloon and Eatery, and you'll feel like you've stepped back to the 1890s. From the bar backdrop, which originated in the Pillsbury Mansion, to the stained-glass chandeliers, the décor is Minnesota-made by craftsmen and artisans. To get the full experience, sit in the corner booth and look out over the floor space below. But be warned, you might not find yourself alone.

The current Last Turn Saloon occupies the basement level of the Model Hotel and Laundry. Built in 1909, it is deemed one of the "most haunted" buildings in downtown Brainerd. Late at night, the old-fashioned phone booth rings, even though it has been disconnected for decades. Men with top hats mysteriously appear next to the end booth. Order Last Turn's creamy beer cheese soup with a side of popcorn. You'll have perfect spirit viewing from the corner booth.

Last Turn Saloon and Eatery, 214 S 8th St., Brainerd
(218) 829-4856

Lake Theatre
Photo courtesy of Vicki Foss

# MUSIC AND ENTERTAINMENT

# START YOUR HOLIDAYS
## AT THE CHRISTMAS CITY
## OF THE NORTH PARADE

It's the most attended public parade in the Northwoods, and one of our oldest. For over six decades, the Christmas City of the North Parade has ushered in the holiday season. Held the Friday before Thanksgiving, this parade offers plenty of holiday action, including marching bands, dance performances, dignitaries, brightly lit floats, and an appearance by Saint Nicholas himself.

The Christmas City of the North Parade starts at 6 p.m. and lasts several hours. So, don your Mukluks (#86) and grab a thermos of hot cocoa.

Christmas City of the North Parade
www.visitduluth.com

**TIP**
Stay at Fitger's Hotel for the weekend
to avoid parking issues and traffic.

# ATTEND
# LIVE ENTERTAINMENT
## WITH CENTRAL LAKES
## COLLEGE PERFORMING ARTS

Looking for something fun to do this month? Central Lakes College Performing Arts Center has some kind of wonderful waiting just for you. From talented local community performers honing their craft in *The Marvelous Wonderettes* to international artists such as Tonic Sol-fa, your need for laughter, tears, and surprises will be satisfied year-round. Outdoor drive-in movie nights were popular in 2020, adding a touch of family nostalgia for summer visitors.

Three separate venues are used for indoor performances. The Chalberg Theatre seats 270 people including a spacious wheel chair accessible area. Guests get up close and personal in the Dryden Theatre which seats up to 130 guests in a black-box style space. Larger performances are held at the historic Tornstrom Auditorium in the Washington Educational Services Building on Oak Street in Brainerd. Order your tickets early to avoid missing out on live action in an intimate setting.

Central Lakes College Performing Arts Center, 501 W College Dr., Brainerd
(218) 855-8199, clcperformingarts.com

# FIND YOUR GROOVE
## AT THE BAYFRONT BLUES FESTIVAL

Duluth's Bayfront Blues Festival draws over 7,000 attendees annually, and about 90 percent of those are returnees. It's the largest outdoor blues festival in the upper Midwest. What's the lure? Two stages and late-night dance parties encourage music lovers of all ages to find their groove and enjoy the country's favorite blues musicians. Artists include the Lamont Cranston Blues Band, Jack Knife & The Sharps, Randy McAllister, and a host of regional blues bands.

In addition to great music, this festival offers regional food vendors, cool merchandise, and an amazing view. It's located on the harbor side of Duluth's Lake Superior Port, so you can listen to music and watch the ships come in at the same time. It's the perfect way to spend an August weekend.

Bayfront Blues Festival, Bayfront Festival Park, Duluth
(218) 722-4011, bayfrontblues.com

# TIP

The Bayfront Blues Festival is an outdoor event, so pack your sunscreen, sunglasses, folding chair, and binoculars. The nearby harbor walk is beautiful if you need a few minutes to stretch your legs.

# GET SCARED
## AT HAUNTED HIDDEN HOLLOWS

Each fall, when the cornstalks rustle in the breeze and Halloween approaches, Paul Bunyan Land transforms from an amusement park to Haunted Hidden Hollows. It's enough to scare the YELL out of anyone. The haunted corn maze is rebuilt every year and encompasses up to 14 acres. If you dare, the haunted house and tractor ride will make you scream, "Enough!" before the night is over. Eerie sights and sounds accompany great visual effects.

A talented Scare Crew volunteer year after year for just one purpose: to give visitors the scare of their lives. This Halloween spectacular is not recommended for the weak of heart or small children.

Haunted Hidden Hollows, 17553 MN-18, Brainerd
(218) 764-2524, paulbunyanland.com

---

### TIP
If you're not into the scare scene, Paul Bunyan Land is open Memorial Day weekend through Labor Day with great family activities, including a 26-foot-tall Paul Bunyan statue that welcomes children by name.

# TAKE IN A PERFORMANCE
## AT THE HISTORIC CHIEF THEATER

The Chief Theater stands as a testament of a bygone era—the wonderful olden days of movie houses. Today, the updated art deco building is home of the Paul Bunyan Playhouse and the Bemidji Community Theater. The Paul Bunyan Playhouse, the longest continuously running summer stock company in Minnesota, draws actors from across the country. Each summer, from June into August, live performers take the stage. The rest of the year, curated entertainment from around the world is offered, including radio shows. To pay honor to the Chief Theater's earliest years, movie nights were brought back in 2016.

The Chief Theater's website lists performances from 1951 through the current year. Classics such as *An Inspector Calls* and *Dial M for Murder* are played on the same stage as *Hairspray* and *Altar Boyz*. You'll laugh and cry, yell and sigh at the Historic Chief Theater.

Chief Theater, 314 Beltrami Ave. NW, Bemidji
(218) 751-7270, thechieftheater.com

# DANCE
## AT LAKES JAM

Lakes Jam unites nationally renowned rock and country bands on two stages the first weekend of August. Located at the Brainerd International Raceway (#59), Jammers hunker down for three days of music and entertainment. Seasoned Jammers recommend getting the VIP package and a three-day camping pass. The VIP pass gives patrons access to front-stage viewing, tap beverages, a covered dining room, exclusive restrooms, and special perks. The camping pass reduces the chance of missing your favorite band, but adds serious steps to your day.

Upcoming entertainers include Carly Pearce, Larry Fleet, Sailor Jerri, Eric Chesser, Slaughter, Ledfoot Larry, Dayna Koehn, and more. Order your tickets online early for the best prices and seating.

Lakes Jam, 5523 Birchdale Rd., Brainerd

# TIP

Bring your lawn chair, bug spray, earplugs, and beverages in plastic containers. Check online for restrictions before you head out.

# BRING IN THE HOLIDAYS
## WITH CONCORDIA COLLEGE'S HOLIDAY CONCERT

This year, get out of your PJs, turn off the holiday carols on the radio, and head to Concordia College for an Emmy Award-winning Christmas concert. The first weekend of December, four choir ensembles and a symphony orchestra combine to create the beautiful holiday music you're craving. At times, the concert hall is so quiet, you can hear a pin drop, which is quite a feat for a group of over 300 singers. Then, their voices reach maximum velocity, and you find yourself sitting on the edge of your seat. The grand finale, "Peace, Peace," will give you goosebumps.

Yearly themes make every year special. Get your tickets early. They go on sale the first week of November for the concert.

Concordia College's Holiday Concert, 901 8th St. S, Moorhead
(888) 477-0277, concordiacollege.edu/music/christmas-concert

---

**TIP**
Stop by the Hjemkomst Center and see the full-size replica of the *Gokstad* Viking ship discovered in Norway in 1880.

# RIDE IN A HORSE-DRAWN CARRIAGE
## BY DULUTH'S WATERFRONT

You've toured the Duluth Harbor by train, helicopter, and boat, but have you tried by carriage? Top Hat Carriages awaits your arrival with Cinderella-size carriages (large enough for six people) pulled by stately, sure-footed horses. Tours range from 20 to 90 minutes in length. The 90-minute ride takes guests to Leif Erikson Park and back. You'll see the downtown in a different perspective—one that takes riders back to a slower, simpler time.

Evening rides are magical and romantic. The end of the tour takes you past the iconic Aerial Lift Bridge, which glows with golden lights. A carriage ride is the perfect place to propose to your special someone from Memorial Day into October.

Duluth Harbor Carriage Rides
Top Hat Carriages, Canal Park
(507) 438-2164, tophatcarriages.com

# CELEBRATE
## BOB DYLAN

Robert Allen Zimmerman was born in Duluth and raised on the Iron Range in Hibbing. After high school, Robert took the name Bob Dylan and became one of the greatest singer-songwriters of the 20th century. His civil rights-era music prompted thousands of young adults to become activists for life.

Every summer, Hibbing celebrates their hometown superstar with Dylan Days. Emerging writers, musicians, and artists join together to highlight Dylan's music. His childhood home still stands—it was purchased by a superfan who is renovating the house to its 1950s appearance. Although 2475 7th Avenue is not open for tours, there is a small sign posted in the yard.

Duluth also claims Dylan as their own and celebrates Dylan Fest in late May. The Bob Dylan Way exhibit can be viewed all year at Fitger's Complex (#12).

Bob Dylan Celebrations and Festivals
bobdylanway.com, dylandays.org

# WATCH A MOVIE
## AT LAKE THEATRE

Chow down on Poor Gary's chicken wild rice pizza (#1) and enjoy a cold beer on Moose Lake Brewery's patio (#5) before experiencing the small-town charm of Lake Theatre. Five generations of the Lower family have greeted patrons at the door of this 308-seat, single-screen theatre. The friendly staff, modern seating, and air-conditioning make hot summer evenings more enjoyable for cabin-goers. To get the full effect, order a large buttered popcorn and soda before you sit down.

This little theater is packed with nostalgia. From the candy counter to the lobby lighting, theater goers will get a glimpse of the olden days of movie theaters. Lake Theater shows include favorites like *Ghostbusters* and new releases.

Lake Theatre, 320 Elm Ave., Moose Lake
(218) 485-4395, mooselaketheater.com

# VISIT
## BEMIDJI'S WATERMARK ART CENTER

The Watermark Art Center houses four galleries of exhibits, with something for every interest and every age. Native American art, contemporary art, juried exhibits, live workshops, historical displays, and educational opportunities are some of the offerings featured all year. Rotating exhibits keep the galleries fresh and interesting.

Craft-at-home kits are sold for both children and adults to extend their art appreciation. The kits are a great way to introduce art to children on rainy days up north. The Watermark Art Center also coordinates a First Friday Art Walk with area businesses and artists to showcase local talents. Each month, different artists participate, so it's worth your time to take in several.

Watermark Art Center, 505 Bemidji Ave. N, Bemidji
(218) 444-7570, watermarkartcenter.org

# SEE JUDY GARLAND'S RUBY SLIPPERS
## AT THE JUDY GARLAND MUSEUM

There's no place like home, or so Judy Garland said in *The Wizard of Oz*. The Judy Garland Museum in Grand Rapids is home to the largest collection of *The Wizard of Oz* memorabilia. In 2005, the museum's pair of Dorothy's ruby slippers were stolen, only to be returned in 2018. I'm sure the shoes are glad to be home.

Garland's childhood home has been restored and is part of two acres of family fun. Visitors can view the iconic Lincoln Carriage (pulled by a horse of a different color) and explore the Children's Discovery Museum. Check out their website for special showings of movie clips and upcoming events. Watch out for flying monkeys!

Judy Garland Museum, 2727 Pokegama Ave. S, Grand Rapids
(218) 327-9276, judygarlandmuseum.com

---

### TIP
A must do activity while touring the Judy Garland Museum is taking a family photo on the Yellow Brick Road. Will you be the Cowardly Lion or brave Dorothy? Why choose? Try them all!

# DANCE
## AT ISKIGAMIZIGAN POWWOW

The Mille Lacs Band of the Ojibwe celebrated the 100th anniversary of the first Jingle Dress in 2019. The story of the Jingle Dress traces back to the global pandemic of 1918–1919, and brought healing to the Ojibwe people. The jingles on women's dresses were originally made from snuff cans rolled into a cylinder and sewn onto their dresses. The familiar jingle is a reminder of the strength of the culture and history of the Ojibwe tribes.

Minnesota Northwoods is home to seven Ojibwe reservations, and many of them hold annual powwows. The Mille Lacs Iskigamizigan Powwow occurs in mid-August and features traditional dancing, drumming, colorful regalia (including Jingle Dresses), food, crafts, games, and a day full of sharing culture. For the best experience, bring your own chair and follow powwow etiquette.

Iskigamizigan Powwow, millelacsband.com

# HEAR POET LAUREATES
## AT VERSE LIKE WATER

The Minnesota Northwoods is not where most poetry lovers would expect to meet Charles Simic, Billy Simons, or William Merlin. However, Jeff Johnson (organizer extraordinaire) has brought these and many other national and international poets to center stage at Central Lakes College for over a decade. Johnson hosts Verse Like Water though in-kind donations and a considerable amount of grant writing. Poets give an hour-long reading of their work as well as free workshops, and take time to answer audience questions. The attendees are only asked to open their hearts to the possibility of poetry.

Verse Like Water events are held in the Chalberg Theatre, which has ample seating and is climate-controlled. Upcoming poets are posted on the website. Johnson usually hosts three to four poets a year, and each year is a must-see event for poetry lovers.

Verse Like Water, 501 W College Dr., Brainerd
(320) 260-4959, clcmn.edu/vlw

# DISCOVER
# MUSIC AND ART
## IN THE PARK

In communities across the Northwoods, summer is the perfect time to share music and art. We love to gather in parks and green spaces. Music and Art in the Park events range from just one day to weekly summer occurrences. Listed below are several events. More can be found on local Chamber of Commerce calendars.

Crosby Music in the Park Series
Thursdays in summer: www.cuyuna.com

Music in Gregory Park
Thursdays in summer: www.visitbrainerd.com

Pequot Lakes Bands in the Park
Summer: www.pequotlakes-mn.gov

Pine City Art in the Park
June and July: www.pinecitychamber.com

For the most listings, please go to www.exploreminnesota.com.

# FIND POLKA MUSIC, FOOD, AND BEER
## AT OKTOBERFESTS

People of German descent, and people who just love German culture, enjoy monthlong Oktoberfests in the Northwoods. The festivities usually begin the last weekend of September, when microbreweries tap their first kegs of their fall varieties and restaurants break open the bratwurst and sauerkraut. Some notable celebrations include the Oktoberfest in Duluth, with three weeks of authentic food, beer, and music at all Grandma's restaurant locations.

Ruttger's Bay Lake Lodge in Deerwood hosts thousands of visitors the third weekend of October. Oktoberfest has taken place at Ruttger's for over 35 years. With that kind of experience, they have created quite a following. Beer, authentic food, polka music, entertainment tents, and a 160-booth craft show make it a weekend of family fun. For the best German Oktoberfest experience, book your room in advance.

grandmasrestaurants.com
ruttgers.com/oktoberfest

# TOUR THE LIGHTS
## AT BENTLEYVILLE

Get ready for one of the largest free-walking holiday lights displays in America. Bentleyville Tour of Lights begins setting up in September. By Thanksgiving, thousands of lights are in place for a bright nightly celebration. Your eyes will be dazzled at the intricate light patterns as they dance across Bayfront Festival Park. The full walk-through takes 30-60 minutes, depending on how many warm-ups you need at the firepits. The grand finale is meeting Santa. Please dress accordingly, as this is Minnesota—gloves are a must most years. Cost and hours of operation are on their website. Due to COVID-19, the 2020 Tour of Lights was drive-through only.

Bentleyville Tour of Lights, 704 W Railroad St., Duluth
bentleyvilleusa.org

---

### TIP
If Bentleyville sounds a bit chilly for you, head south to the Butkiewicz Family Farm (#4) for a drive-through holiday light display.

---

# MEET SPOOKS
## ON THE HAUNTED *IRVIN* SHIP

A door slams on the historic iron ore ship. Was it part of the October act, or did you just encounter one of the spirits of the *William A. Irvin*? You'll never know for sure on this self-guided tour through one of the spookiest water vessels on the Great Lakes. The tour begins in the engine room and wraps its way up through the ship. Dark hallways, squeaky doors, and flickering lights are just the beginning. Mysterious spirits show themselves and taunt your nerves. Will you make it out alive?

For those of us not brave enough to tour the *Irvin* in October, regular-season tours take place from May to September.

William A. Irvin Museum, 301 Harbor Dr., Duluth
(218) 722-7876, duluthhauntedship.com

---

### TIP
The Vista Fleet (behind the William A. Irvin) offers tours of the Harbor and Lake Superior. Feel the gales of the big lake while viewing the busy, Great Lakes shipping industry.

# EXPERIENCE
## STAGE NORTH THEATRE COMPANY'S ORIGINAL PRODUCTIONS

Stage North Theatre Company offers affordable, live community theater productions in the Brainerd Lakes Area three to four times a year. In 2018, the original musical, *Baby Face*, brought patrons back to the 1933 First National Bank robbery. History buffs watched as the reenactment came to life with laughter and suspense. The historic Franklin Arts Center theater is the perfect backdrop for productions.

Playwright Roger Nieboer is working on Stage North's *Paul Bunyan: The Myth, The Legend, The Musical* for Brainerd's sesquicentennial in the summer of 2021. *A Christmas Story* appears on stage in December 2021. Sold-out performances are common. Be sure to check the website for dates, show times, and seat availability.

Stage North Theatre Company, 1001 Kingwood St., Brainerd
(218) 232-6810, stagenorththeater.com

# CATCH LIVE MUSIC
## AT WUSSOW'S CONCERT CAFÉ

What do you get when you combine live music, locally produced food and beverages, and a seriously awesome espresso bar? You get Wussow's Concert Café. Located on Central Avenue in Duluth, this is the place for musicians, writers, and everyone else to meet in an inclusive atmosphere. It's a popular place for the over-19 crowd to refuel on friendships, music, and nourishment after work. From breakfast through early evening, Wussow's Concert Café is ready to serve you.

Wussow's Concert Café, 324 N Central Ave., Duluth
(218) 624-5957, wussows.com

### TIP
Grab a Wussow's Concert Café Hoodie and winter hat to keep the chilly Lake Superior wind off your back.

Rock climbing at Banning State Park
Photo courtesy of Vicki Foss

# SPORTS AND RECREATION

# INTERACT WITH ANIMALS
## AT SAFARI NORTH WILDLIFE PARK

Kids of all ages will enjoy interacting with wildlife from around the globe. Hold a stick dipped in bird seed and watch the colorful parakeets land on your arm. Take a ride on Nick the camel, or feed carrots by hand to Jigsaw the giraffe. Safari North offers a petting zoo, gemstones mining, a snack shack, and more for the young as well as the young at heart. Up-close and personal interactions with over 100 exhibits set this animal experience apart from the others.

The staff, zookeepers, and owners Kevin and Kelly Vogel are available to answer questions and share their favorite animal experiences. New in 2020, the snow leopards exhibit dazzled visitors. The Safari North Wildlife Park is open from early May until late September. Seasonal passes are a great way to see the animals weekly. And, their gift shop is amazing!

Safari North Wildlife Park, 8493 State Hwy 371, Brainerd
(218) 454-1662, safarinorth.com

# WADE ACROSS THE MISSISSIPPI HEADWATERS
## IN ITASCA STATE PARK

The mighty Mississippi River begins in Itasca State Park and ends in the Gulf of Mexico, approximately 2,500 miles away. At its source, the river moves so slowly, adults can safely walk across the boulder-strewn path. But be cautious—underwater boulders are covered with algae and can be slippery. Water that flows from Itasca State Park takes three months to reach the gulf.

This is Minnesota's oldest state park and one of the largest, covering 32,000 acres. Overnight camping is available, but sites fill up fast. You will need a state park sticker to access the park by motorized vehicle. Buy the yearly pass, which can be used at all 66 Minnesota State Parks. Hiking, biking, and water sports are favorite activities while at Itasca State Park.

Itasca State Park, 36750 Main Park Dr., Park Rapids
(218) 266-2100, stateparks.com/itasca_state_park_in_minnesota.html

---

**TIP**
Don't forget to pack water shoes, a canteen, and a snack. Hiking sticks are especially helpful for uneven terrain.

# CANOE
## THE BOUNDARY WATERS CANOE AREA

This one should be on everyone's bucket list. *National Geographic* named the BWCA one of 50 must-see destinations of a lifetime. Trips to the Boundary Waters require careful planning, the right equipment, and a permit. New BWCA visitors are encouraged to use a guide or travel with a seasoned friend, especially if fishing or canoeing to a specific lake. With one million acres of wilderness—and limited cellphone coverage—you want to be ready for adventure.

Outfitters such as Piragis Northwoods Company (#97) can supply you with high-quality, dependable equipment that will last for many years. Bring a few extra pairs of socks and a good camera. Common wildlife sightings include moose, wolves, bears, beavers, eagles, and many more.

Boundary Waters Canoe Area
bwca.com

### TIP
Check local fire danger warnings and campfire restrictions before you leave on your trip. Only you can prevent forest fires!

# BIKE
## AT CUYUNA LAKES MOUNTAIN BIKE TRAILS AND CUYUNA LAKES STATE TRAIL SYSTEM

Mountain bikers leave the trails exhilarated and covered with telltale red soil-stained sneakers. Trails snake around iron ore mines, now turned into freshwater lakes. Novice bikers leave the Cuyuna Lakes Mountain Bike Trails with fresh scrapes, cuts, and bumps—and a commitment to ride again.

The Cuyuna Lakes State Trail is part of the Cuyuna Country State Recreation Area. It provides eight miles of paved trail and several levels of difficulty. To access these trails, you will need a state park sticker on your vehicle. State Park stickers are available at Minnesota State Parks or online. Yearly passes are a great way to see all of the Northwoods State Parks and Recreation Areas.

Cuyuna Lakes Mountain Biking, 17934 Co. Rd. 30, Ironton
cuyunalakesmtb.com

---

**TIP**
Pack a swimsuit and towel in your backpack.
The cool lake water will feel great after hitting the trails.

---

# WATCH HAWKS
## AT HAWK RIDGE BIRD OBSERVATORY

You don't have to be a certified ornithologist to take part in the raptor counts at Hawk Ridge. Every spring, raptors fly from as far south as South America, past Lake Superior, on their way north. Some raptors will continue to the Arctic, often resting in the East Bluffs near Duluth. In fall, the migration pattern is reversed. Twenty different types of raptors and vultures make the annual migrations. Rare sightings include peregrine falcons and gyrfalcons.

The staffed observatory has a list of birds currently migrating and also information on sponsoring a release (you actually hold the bird and release it into the air!) A good day to see the raptors usually includes a northwest wind and relatively clear skies.

Hawk Ridge Bird Observatory, 3980 E Skyline Parkway, Duluth
(218) 428-6209, hawkridge.org

# TIP

Spring raptor counts run from March until May. Fall raptor counts take place from August 15 until November 30. Bring a good pair of binoculars and a folding chair.

# WIN A TRUCK
## AT THE JAYCEES ICE FISHING EXTRAVAGANZA

Looking for the largest charitable ice fishing contest in the world? Look no further than Gull Lake the last weekend of January. The Jaycees Ice Fishing Extravaganza is "the big one," with over $150,000 in prizes and more than 700 participants from across the country. Ice fishing participants compete for prize packages based on the size and ranking of their fish. In 2020, the top fish was an 8.29-pound eelpout. Prizes range from new trucks to the latest ice fishing rods.

The funds raised from the Friday Night Kick-Off Party are given to the Brainerd Warrior Fishing Team. Tickets are purchased online for Friday and Saturday's events; guidelines are strictly adhered to. Proceeds on Saturday benefit the Confidence Learning Center. If you choose to participate or watch, warming houses are available. But be warned—you cannot catch fish from warming houses.

Jaycees Ice Fishing Extravaganza, Hole in the Bay Day, Gull Lake
icefishing.org

# TIP

Wear your Mukluks and insulated pants. Area lakes are perfect for ice fishing from December through February. Call the Minnesota Department of Natural Resources for lake conditions.

# SEE BEARS UP CLOSE
## AT THE VINCE SHUTE WILDLIFE SANCTUARY

In the middle of the Northwoods, this is your safest option to get up close and personal with lots of black bears all at once. Visitors are driven to a fenced-in treehouse, and the bears come to you. I won't spoil the fun but will repeat that you'll see bears at the sanctuary. Stop by the gift shop for a memento of your favorite bear.

Vince Shute Wildlife Sanctuary, 12541 Nett Lake Rd., Orr
(218) 757-0172, americanbear.org

### TIP
For best viewing, visit the Vince Shute Bear Sanctuary in the evening.

# JOIN ROCK HOUNDS
## AT MINNESOTA NORTHWOODS ROCK AND GEM SHOWS

Some people will debate me on this one, but my fellow rock hounds agree: Agate hunting is a form of recreation. Winter is the only season we take a break from searching the shores of Lake Superior or farm fields for agates. By spring, many of us are suffering from withdrawal. Along come rock and gem shows! The Cuyuna Gem and Mineral Show is held Mother's Day weekend and offers a variety of nature-made rocks, gemstones, and minerals. Some are raw, while others have been polished and inserted into jewelry, tables, and crafts. Over 100 vendors participate each year, and show organizers take care to have projects for children.

In mid-July, the small town of Moose Lake hosts Moose Lake Agate Days, another large show which includes a real agate stampede. Several city blocks are roped off, and truckloads of rocks, agates, and quarters are dropped. Pickers from across the country come to try their luck. Everyone leaves with a few rocks and a smile on their face.

Cuyuna Gem and Mineral Show, Crow Wing County Fair Grounds
cuyunarockclub.org

Moose Lake Agate Days Gem and Mineral Show, Moose Lake
mooselakechamber.com

# SCORE A HOLE IN ONE
## ON A PROFESSIONAL-GRADE GOLF COURSE

Golf is a sport that is popular in the Northwoods. Courses listed below offer an assortment of challenges, even for the best golfers. If you read professional golf magazines, you'll recognize the following as part of Minnesota's Top 10! Grab your golf cart and clubs—your tee time is approaching.

Giant's Ridge (The Quarry and The Legend), Biwabik
(218) 865-8042, (218) 865-8000, giantsridge.com

The Wilderness at Fortune Bay, Tower
(218) 753-8917, golfthewilderness.com

Breezy Point Resort – Deacon's Lodge, Brainerd
(218) 562-6262, breezypoint.com

The Preserve Golf Course at Grand View Lodge, Nisswa
(218) 568-4944, grandviewlodge.com

The Classic at Madden's Golf Course, Brainerd
(218) 829-2811, maddens.com

# WATCH
## THE JOHN BEARGREASE SLED DOG MARATHON

John Beargrease is a legend on the Northshore. His dedication to delivering mail through rain, sleet, and snow are celebrated for three weeks in January, ending with the big 400-mile John Beargrease Sled Dog Marathon. The Beargrease is the longest sled dog race in the lower 48 states and is a qualifier for Alaska's Iditarod. It tests the endurance of both mushers and their sled dogs.

Cub Runs, Mini Sled Dog Races, a Cutest Puppy Contest, and BrewSheen are just a few of the events leading up to the marathon. Starting places and dates occasionally change due to Minnesota weather conditions. Please check the website frequently for updates.

The John Beargrease Sled Dog Marathon, 218 W Superior St., Duluth
(218) 461-1834, beargrease.com

### TIP
If you have children, you'll want to check out the neat educational material available through the website.

# GET SPLASHED
## AT GOOSEBERRY FALLS STATE PARK

The Gooseberry River creates quite a splash and ROARS as it plummets through the High, Middle, and Lower Falls into the rocky gorge below. The view from above is breathtaking, and can be a bit wet after heavy rains. Watch your footing and wear good shoes.

If heights are not your passion, hike to the Fifth Falls and enjoy a picnic lunch next to Lake Superior. Gooseberry Falls is considered the gateway to the Northshore and has camping sites available. They fill up months in advance, so reserve your site early. You will need a state park sticker to access Gooseberry Falls by motorized vehicle.

Gooseberry Falls State Park, 3206 MN-61, Two Harbors
(218) 595-7100, dnr.state.mn.us/state_parks

## TIP
A word of caution, be very careful crossing the bridge and Highway 61. Traffic moves at a good clip in the summer and the sun can make seeing pets and small children difficult.

# COUNT BIRDS
## AT THE ANNUAL SAX ZIM BOG BIRDING FESTIVAL

The Sax Zim Bog is a strange birding phenomenon. It's a hot spot for birds of all varieties, including great grey owls, boreal owls, and eagles. Every Presidents Day weekend, 150 birders from across the region register for the annual birding festival. Birding is practiced throughout the year near the bog due to the abundance of wildlife. Grab your binoculars, a thermos of hot cocoa, and bird identification book for a day of bird enjoyment.

Sax Zim Bog Birding Festival, Meadowlands
saxzimbirdingfestival.com

### TIP
When vole populations are low in Canada, Snowy Owls will head south to the Sax Zim Bog for food. In late December of 2020, birders flocked to the bog to see these majestic owls.

# GET ACTIVE
## ON THE PAUL BUNYAN TRAIL

The Paul Bunyan Trail covers 120 miles, from Crow Wing State Park (#81) north to Bemidji. The paved trail is handicap-accessible and perfect for all-season recreation, including hiking, bicycling, rollerblading, snowmobiling, snowshoeing, walking, and geocaching. The trail goes through 14 Northwoods communities, and has rest stops along the way. Grab a friend and get moving. Maps are available at area businesses or on the website below.

Paul Bunyan Trail
paulbunyantrail.com

## TIP
Savor a piece of cheesecake at Bites Grill & Bar. Refill your water bottle and you'll be good for many more miles. And don't forget—safety first. Along with your water bottle, a helmet and first aid kit make long rides more enjoyable.

# EXPLORE
## THE US HOCKEY
## HALL OF FAME MUSEUM

Eveleth is a small town that has produced more than its share of quality hockey players. Because of its rich hockey tradition, it was designated as the capital of American hockey. Twelve Eveleth natives have been inducted into the US Hockey Hall of Fame, including Doug Palazzari, John Mariucci, and Willard Ikola. Minnesota as a whole has produced an abundance of Hall of Fame players. Hockey also has huge fan support from Minnesota Northwoods residents. Fans are a big part of the Hockey Hall of Fame Museum.

Hockey fans can have their pictures taken with a giant hockey stick, sit on sections of their favorite stadium seats, and check out old-time hockey safety equipment. There are plenty of photographs, taped interviews, and news clips to look at, too. If you consider yourself a hockey buff, you need to explore the US Hockey Hall of Fame Museum for yourself.

US Hockey Hall of Fame Museum, 801 Hat Trick Ave., Eveleth
(218) 744-5167, ushockeyhall.com

# HIKE ACROSS
# THE SWINGING BRIDGE
## AT JAY COOKE STATE PARK

The Jay Cooke State Park swinging suspension bridge stretches high above the St. Louis River. Crossing it can make your stomach jump. On one side of the bridge are amenities such as the gift shop and bathrooms. The other side embraces wilderness and is home to spectacular spring wildflowers. Active visitors often hike, backpack, bike, ski, and horseback ride in the park. Jay Cooke has beautiful picnic grounds, so don't forget to pack a lunch—though you might want to wait to eat until after you cross the bridge! A state park sticker is required to enter the park.

Cemetery lovers, the Thompson Pioneer Cemetery is located within the park grounds. The oldest headstone is dated 1862. The markers have deteriorated through the years; however, several are visible. The state park map is helpful to locate the cemetery.

Jay Cooke State Park, 780 MN-210, Carlton
(218) 673-7000, dnr.state.mn

# WALK UP
# TO THE HIGH FALLS
## AT GRAND PORTAGE STATE PARK

Minnesota might be home to dozens of waterfalls, but none can compare to the High Falls at Grand Portage State Park. Reaching a height of 120 feet, the Pigeon River plunges down with a mighty roar. Three viewing decks give ample opportunity to photograph the falls or meditate in awe. I found the Middle Falls quite stunning and especially enjoyed the view of Lake Superior from the park's highest point. If you choose to hike to the Middle Falls, wear good walking shoes and bring a water bottle. Also, the five-mile hike can be challenging in the heat of August. You will need a Minnesota State Parks sticker to enter the park.

Grand Portage State Park, Grand Portage
(218) 475-2360, dnr.state.mn.us

### TIP
The Pigeon River and High Falls are shared between the US and Canada. Cross the border and view the falls from the Canadian side for a different perspective.

# FEEL THE BREEZE
## AS YOU DOWNHILL SKI

Minnesota winters can last four to six months, which makes the Northwoods great downhill skiing country. The Northshore's Sawtooth Mountains provide exceptional ski runs and first-class ski resorts. Lutsen Mountains has the largest vertical drop at 825 feet. Skiers and snowboarders enjoy the winter resort ambiance and the outstanding views. Duluth's Spirit Mountain's vertical drop is an impressive 700 feet and also provides great views of Lake Superior. Four freestyle terrains provide space for practicing smooth moves.

Other Northwoods skiing destinations of note are Giants Ridge in Biwabik, Mt. Itasca Winter Sports Center near Grand Rapids, and Mount Ski Gull in Nisswa. Tubing, snowshoeing, and skiing are great ways to pass the long winter and remain active outdoors.

**Lutsen Mountains**
476 Ski Hill Rd., Lutsen
(218) 663-7281, lutsen.com

**Spirit Mountain Recreation Area**
9500 Spirit Mountain Pl, Duluth
(218) 628-2891, spiritmt.com

**Giants Ridge Recreation Area**
6329 Wynne Creek Dr., Biwabik
(218) 865-8000, giantsridge.com

**Mt. Itasca Winter Sport Center**
200 Mount Itasca Dr., Coleraine
(218) 245-3487, mtitasca.com

**Mt. Ski Gull**
9898 County 77 SW, Nisswa
(218) 963-4353, mountskigull.com

# GET YOUR HEART RACING
## AT BRAINERD INTERNATIONAL RACEWAY

Start your engines and experience the very best professional racing with the Lucas Oil NHRA Nationals featuring the world's best drag racers. This high-energy race occurs every August and sports the fastest cars, best drivers, and four days of racing excitement for fans. Youngsters love to watch teams tear down and rebuild their cars, smell the nitro, and collect their favorite drivers' autographs. At the end of the day, night life begins. Adults listen to bands, chat by bonfires, and grab great race food at the Zoo campground.

BIR also hosts drifting and superbike racing throughout the summer months. Ready to try racing for yourself? Enroll in the BIR Performance Driving School. You'll learn to take turns like a pro on a real race track.

Brainerd International Raceway, 5523 Birchdale Rd., Brainerd
(866) 444-4455, brainredraceway.com

### TIP
Before heading to the track, get a pair of quality earplugs and a cushion for the bleachers. Once you try BIR, you'll be back again and again.

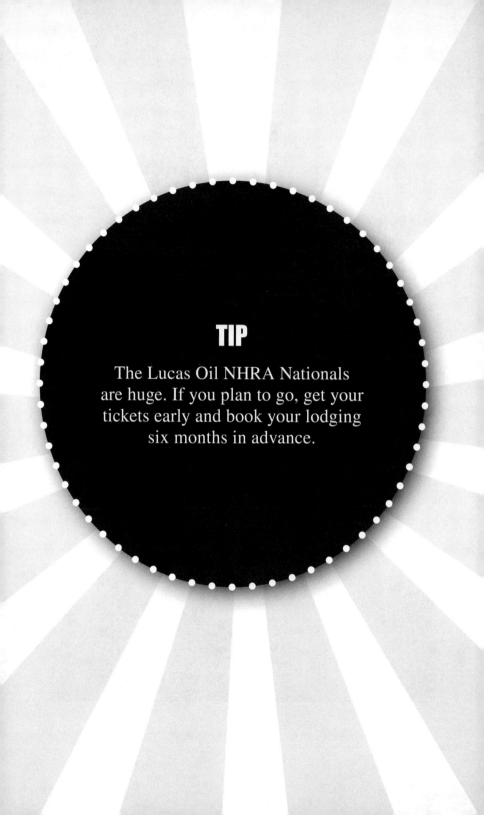

# TIP

The Lucas Oil NHRA Nationals
are huge. If you plan to go, get your
tickets early and book your lodging
six months in advance.

# HIKE
## AT FRITZ LOVEN PARK

Fritz Loven Park is a hidden gem of the Brainerd Lakes Area. The park is named after a lifelong bachelor who settled on the land in the 1930s. Loven passed away in 1975, and a year later, his sister sold his property to the city of Lake Shore. The park offers year-round recreation, including a trout stream, handicap fishing pier, snowshoe trails, and Nordic ski trails. Picnic shelters, restrooms, and a playground make Fritz Loven a peaceful family retreat 365 days a year.

Fritz Loven Park, 7877 Ridge Rd., Lake Shore

### TIP
Buy a trout and salmon stamp when you purchase your Minnesota Fishing License in the spring. You can use it all year across the state. Northwoods convenience stores, bait and tackle shops, and outdoor supply retailers can set you up with single or family licenses.

# RIDE, BIKE, OR HIKE
## SCENIC HIGHWAY 61

Scenic Highway 61, also called the North Shore Drive, was the dream of Chester Congdon (#67). His financial backing and careful planning were instrumental to this beautiful highway.

Scenic Highway 61 stretches from just north of Duluth to the Canada border. The highway is dotted with towns, restaurants, and rest areas. It is the perfect recreational roadway.

Competitive and leisure bicyclists enjoy the challenge of the hills. Tourists savor the view of Lake Superior throughout the year. In spring, lupines cover the roadside, creating picture-perfect scenery. Throughout summer, wayside rests offer easy access to the shores of Lake Superior. Maple, oak, and birch trees display show-stopping autumn colors during September and October. The long months of winter are busy with snowmobilers and Nordic skiers traversing the land next to Scenic Highway 61. Exercise your favorite way on Scenic Highway 61.

Scenic Highway 61

# BE AMAZED
## BY THE SKI LOONS WATER SKI SHOW

Water skiing was a favorite pasttime in the Northwoods; after all, we have more water than any other part of Minnesota. Through the years, though, water-skiing shows disappeared, and folks forgot about the intricate formations, teamwork, and confidence building that encompassed the sport. Enter the Brainerd Ski Loons Water Ski Show Team. The team practices and performs on Rice Lake. Public viewing takes place from the shores by Lum Park. Bring your own lawn chair and arrive early, as the Ski Loons have developed a large following. In 2018, over 1,800 people viewed their four shows.

The Ski Loons are known for their big group pyramids, ballet lines, trios, and new formations. Each show adds a bit of wonder to the sport of water skiing.

Brainerd Ski Loons Water Ski Show, 4784 Gull Dam Rd., Brainerd
(218) 831-3290, skiloons.com

# STOCK UP
## AT TUTT'S BAIT & TACKLE

Mille Lacs Lake (#65) covers 207 square miles and is home to trophy-size walleye, muskellunge, bass, and panfish. If you want to catch one of the BIG fish, a stop at Tutt's Bait & Tackle is a must. The building looks small on the outside, but it's packed with everything you need. From the right lure (for your favorite fish) to clothing with built-in sunblock, you'll be ready for a great day on the lake. If you're new to fishing on Mille Lacs Lake, sign up for a Tutt's fishing guide to show you around. They will recommend you check Tutt's website for the most current fishing report. It is updated daily and gives great insight on where the fish are being caught year round.

Buy an assortment of bait and tackle and don't shy away from the big ones. In June 2019, a monster sized muskie was pulled into a DNR boat working on Mille Lacs Lake. The muskie's unofficial measurement of 61.5" beat the world record set in 1949 by over an inch. Big fish like big bait from Tutt's Bait and Tackle.

Tutt's Bait & Tackle, 27358 MN-18, Garrison
(320) 692-4341, tuttsbaitandtackle.com

# CLIMB A ROCK WALL
## AT BANNING STATE PARK

Rock climbing is a popular sport—the lure of reaching new heights can be a real adrenaline rush. Banning State Park near Sandstone offers a special type of climbing called "bouldering." Bouldering occurs on short routes, or "problems," and if you reach the top of the climb, your problem is solved. Climbs range in difficulty from V0 to V11. Start with an easier climb and work your way up to The Raven, a V11. Once you reach the top, enjoy the view and consider your problem solved for the day.

New to rock climbing? Reserve one of Banning State Park's 36 drive-in campsites. You can pace your "bouldering" progression over several days. (Your body will thank you.) When not climbing, swim, hike, bike, kayak, or try your hand at river fishing.

Banning State Park, 61101 Banning Park Rd., Sandstone
(320) 216-3910, dnr.state.mn.us

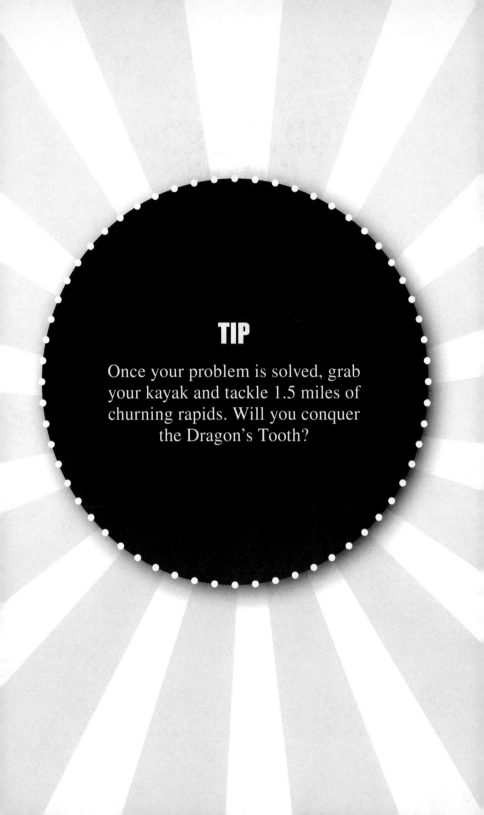

# TIP

Once your problem is solved, grab your kayak and tackle 1.5 miles of churning rapids. Will you conquer the Dragon's Tooth?

# CATCH LEGENDARY WALLEYES
## ON MILLE LACS LAKE

In the "Land of 10,000 Lakes," fishing takes on a competitive note. Mille Lacs Lake is the second largest lake located totally in Minnesota. It's big and shallow, and walleyes seem to thrive in the legendary "walleye chop." Resorts scattered around the lake offer their own landings and amenities. Just stock up on bait before you launch at Tutt's Bait & Tackle (#63). Once you're catching fish, you won't want to come off the lake.

Large walleye like a little chop to the water and this lake is famous for summer chops. One walleye caught on Mille Lacs Lake in 2012 was 33.75" and weighed just shy of 14#. If the walleyes elude your best attempts, switch bait and seek out muskie, Northern pike, bass, or tasty panfish. Walleye aren't the only fish on this big lake.

Mille Lacs Area Tourism Council, 630 W Main St., Isle
(320) 676-9972, millelacs.com

# WHITE WATER RAFT
## WITH SWIFTWATER ADVENTURES

The St. Louis River is the largest river that flows into Lake Superior, and the only river in Minnesota that offers white water rafting. Thrill seekers rush to the Saint Louis to ride the rapids and challenge their abilities. Swiftwater Adventures caters to rafters of all skill levels and provides equipment, instruction, and in-raft guides. You'll learn safety tips to avoid injury as well as what to look for if you want a faster ride. White water rafting is a great adventure for friends and families. Time slots fill up quickly, so schedule your adventure in advance.

Swiftwater Adventures, 121 Vermillion St., Carlton
(218) 451-3218, swiftwatermn.com

### TIP
Stop by Jay Cooke State Park (#56) after your water adventure. You'll be high and dry as you cross the St. Louis River on the swinging bridge.

Lucette in Hackensack
Photo courtesy of Vicki Foss

# CULTURE AND HISTORY

# FIND TREASURES
## ON A GLENSHEEN MANSION TOUR

Glensheen Mansion is the most visited historic home in Minnesota. Since 1979, the University of Minnesota has restored and operated Glensheen as a museum. A tour allows adults a long look at turn-of-the-century grandeur, exquisite décor, furnishings, and craftsmanship. Five floors of the Congdon family's possessions are on display, and tour guides share their knowledge of the early days.

But, what about children? Are they left out of this history lesson? No. Through the *Glensheen Treasure Book*, children are invited to tour the mansion with Tim the Fox as their guide. Throughout the year, staff hide fun treasures, such as elves at Christmas and pumpkins in October, to encourage child participation. Tours are educational and fun for the whole family.

Glensheen Mansion, 3300 London Rd., Duluth
(218) 726-8910, glensheen.org

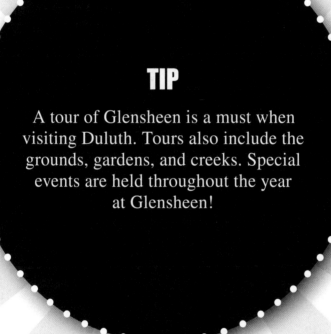

# TIP

A tour of Glensheen is a must when visiting Duluth. Tours also include the grounds, gardens, and creeks. Special events are held throughout the year at Glensheen!

# LEARN OJIBWE CULTURE
## AT MILLE LACS INDIAN MUSEUM

The Mille Lacs Indian Museum weaves together the art and culture of the Ojibwe. Visitors gain a better understanding of the contributions and challenges the Ojibwe people faced in the 1800s and still do today. New in 2020, the Jingle Dress exhibit shares the story of the dress and its meaning to the Ojibwe. The Jingle Dress came to the people through a dream during the 1918–1919 Spanish flu pandemic.

The museum has both permanent and rotating exhibits, all with Ojibwe and English text. Workshops, demonstrations, exhibit scavenger hunts, and children's crafts add to family interactions. In 1960, Mille Lacs Indian Museum became part of the Minnesota Historical Society, which seeks to preserve and share history. The Mille Lacs Indian Museum is one of only 26 Minnesota Historical Society sites and is open seasonally.

Mille Lacs Indian Museum, 43411 Oodena Dr., Onamia
(320) 532-3632, mnhs.org/millelacs

## TIP

A must-see is the Four Seasons Room. Life-size mannequin casts of local Ojibwe tribe members are set in authentic seasonal displays. Recorded narrations and music put viewers in the moment.

# MEET VOYAGEURS
## AT GRAND PORTAGE
## NATIONAL MONUMENT

Throughout the year, the Grand Portage National Monument gives visitors a glimpse into the rich 1800s fur trade. The United States Park Service maintains the site all year, including the Heritage Center, bookstore, archives, exhibits, educational classrooms, and hiking trails.

Land for the monument was donated by the Grand Portage Band of Ojibwe. Every August, Rendezvous Days is held in conjunction with the Grand Portage Ojibwe's Powwow. The huge celebrations take visitors back in time through demonstrations, exhibits, music, and reenactments. Over 300 volunteers gather— many showing their talents in long-forgotten trades. One of my children's favorite activities was listening to the voyageurs converse amongst themselves with friendly bantering. Bring your camera to preserve the history.

Grand Portage National Monument,170 Mile Creek Rd., Grand Portage
(218) 475-0123, nps.gov

### TIP
Take your lunch to the High Falls (#57) and enjoy the roar of Minnesota's largest waterfall.

# SHARE VERBAL HISTORY
## AT THE HARVEST MOON FESTIVAL

Festivals are held throughout the year in the northern part of Minnesota. Food, fun, and fellowship are givens, as is the sharing of verbal history. Ely winters are often harsh; tourism decreases, and snowbirds head to southern states. The weekend after Labor Day, Harvest Moon Festival brings folks together for the final hurrah.

Music flows from Whiteside Park, the Singing Slovenes arrive with their native costumes, and button box players dust off their instruments. Folk musicians from the Iron Range grab their guitars, and polka bands reach for accordions. The atmosphere is relaxed and perfect for meandering through booths of local artist wares, including traditional printing and ceramics. For more information contact ellencashmanevents@ely.org.

Harvest Moon Festival, Ely

# EXPLORE THREE FLOORS OF HISTORY
## AT THE CROW WING COUNTY HISTORICAL SOCIETY MUSEUM

History is well-preserved at the Crow Wing County Historical Society Museum. The museum consists of three floors covered with local artifacts and exhibits. The logging display includes a replica of an 1800s logging camp, tools, and photos. Nearby, the railroad and mining exhibits take viewers through bygone eras. A large research library is the perfect place to complete genealogy. So much to do, so little time.

Speaking of time, the historical society is housed in the original county jail and sheriff's residence. Here, visitors have hands-on access to the kitchen, family rooms, and actual jail cells. Sit on the steel commode or try to rest on the flimsy cot. My favorite part is taking family photos in the slammer for an unforgettable holiday card.

Crow Wing County Historical Society Museum, 320 Laurel, Brainerd
(218) 829-3268, crowwinghistory.org

# CHECK OUT
## THE LAKE SUPERIOR MARINE MUSEUM

You'll appreciate the Great Lakes even more after a visit to the Lake Superior Marine Museum. The museum is operated by the US Army Corps of Engineers. Its location in Canal Park near the Aerial Lift Bridge brings visitors next to the real action. Watch 1,000-foot ships enter and leave the harbor either from within the museum or on the large deck, where you can have the full effect. Listen to ships and the lift bridge "talk" through a series of horns and whistles (this will make you jump the first time you hear it). Ship schedules are posted, so you'll know exactly which ship you're seeing as well as which country it is from.

Interactive displays make the Lake Superior Marine Museum an excellent stop for families with children. A popular display tells the sad story of the *Edmund Fitzgerald* shipwreck. I love seeing the replicas of an early ship's sailors' quarters and passenger room.

Lake Superior Marine Museum, 600 Canal Park Dr., Duluth
(218) 788-6430, lsmma.com

---

### TIP
Tall Ships are the grandest of all ships that ever sailed. These historic beauties can be seen from the Marine Museum in early August.

# FIND
## PAUL BUNYAN(S),
## BABE THE BLUE OX(EN), AND LUCETTE

Paul Bunyan, Babe the Blue Ox, and Paul's wife, Lucette, inhabit many towns in the Minnesota Northwoods. Area lore tells us that our lakes were formed by Paul and Babe stomping around. Each time you find a statue, read how Paul is tied to the community. We all claim him as our own celebrity.

I'll get you started on your search by giving you the first three of over 25 destinations. Paul Bunyan Land (#25) near Brainerd has a 26-foot tall Paul Bunyan that greets visitors by name. A 17-foot Lucette can be found in Hackensack's city park. The largest Paul Bunyan looms in Akeley and is an excellent photo opportunity. Keep track of your sightings and make it a family game on long road trips.

### TIP
Warning: Minnesota's Northwoods takes collecting Paul and Babe souvenirs to an extreme level. You'll find an abundance of these northern gentlemen in gift shops across the area. Cards, trivets, action figures, and ceramics abound.

# LISTEN TO OLD-FASHIONED
## STEAM THRESHERS

Introduce your family to farming done the old-fashioned way. Start with a trip to Paul Bunyan Land (#25) and tour the Pioneer Village. Spend quality time in the Thresher Storage and really look at the machines. Consider the time and energy required to keep early farm equipment running well. When you're finished looking at the 45 different Pioneer Village points of interest, take your knowledge to a new location.

Head to the little community of Rollag during Labor Day weekend for the Western Minnesota Steam Threshers Reunion. Since 1954, owners of threshers, steam engines, and antique farm machines have gathered here to celebrate their past and have fun! Hundreds of demonstrations, such as rope making, baking, and farming techniques, along with interactive exhibits, make this a full weekend.

Paul Bunyan Land, 17553 State Hwy 18, Brainerd
(218) 764-2524, paulbunyanland.com

Western Minnesota Steam Threshers Reunion
(701) 212-2034, rollag.com

# VISIT
# THE HUMPHREY CENTER
## FOR AMERICAN INDIAN STUDIES

Housed in the Skone Family Conservatory within the Jon Hassler Library lies the Humphrey Center for American Indian Studies. The center has interactive kiosks, educational displays, and over 3,000 books and research materials. Original American Indian artifacts are on loan from the Pete Humphrey collection. Many of the items on display are from the Minnesota Ojibwe bands, including a Jingle Dress. The intent of this large collection is to build bridges between Indian and non-Indian cultures through education.

The Humphrey Center for American Indian Studies is open when Central Lakes College classes are in session. Tours are held on special occasions.

The Humphrey Center for American Indian Studies
501 W College Dr., Brainerd
(218) 855-8159, mary.sam@clcmn.edu

# REFLECT
## AT THE MILFORD MINE
## MEMORIAL PARK

Minnesota's worst mining accident occurred at the Milford Mine on February 5, 1924. Forty-one miners lost their lives and became encased in mud and water after the mine shaft collapsed. Seven miners made it out that fateful day. The park has excellent signage explaining the ruins left on the site. The tragic story of the Milford Mine disaster is told through kiosks, a memorial bridge, and many photographs. Visitors are encouraged to walk slowly and read all of the displays.

The park is a day destination for hikers, bikers, and historians. Walking paths, picnic shelters, cooking grilles, and bike racks are part of the ongoing upgrades. I encourage visitors to wear comfortable, old shoes because the red iron-laced soil at the park will stain lighter-colored shoes.

Milford Mine Memorial Park, 26351 Milford Lake, Dr., Crosby
crowwing.us/294/milford-mine-memorial-park

### TIP
Stop by the Soo Line Depot Museum (101 1st St. NE)
in Crosby to view a large selection of artifacts and more photos.

# DISCOVER MILITARY HISTORY
## AT THE MINNESOTA MILITARY MUSEUM

Located at Camp Ripley, the Minnesota Military Museum showcases the experiences of military men and women. Visitors can view the equipment, weapons, uniforms, and personal memorabilia of veterans who were part of our nation's military. Permanent displays include *America at War*, *Forts on the Frontier*, and a half dozen more. Special exhibits rotate and have included a tribute to the 50th anniversary of the Vietnam War. Research assistance is available at the on-site military-themed library, the largest of its kind in the state.

Stop by the Minnesota State Veterans Cemetery on-site. There are over 1,500 burials in the cemetery. The white military markers are placed with precision, giving viewers the feeling that they are at Arlington National Cemetery.

Minnesota Military Museum, 15000 Hwy. 115, Little Falls
(320) 616-6050, mnmilitarymuseum.org

# FIND
## THE LOST 40

A surveying error in 1882 is credited to the Lost 40 Scientific and Natural Area (SNA). The error caused this 144-acre old-growth forest to be incorrectly marked as Coddington Lake on maps. Lucky for us! The Lost 40 SNA's marked trail loop leads visitors past white and red pines that are over 230 years old. Interpretive trail markers and a detailed map explain the terrain.

On the way to the Lost 40 SNA on Highway 46, you'll pass Popple Cemetery, a quaint cemetery located on a beautiful stretch of land. Here lies Herbert Cooper, a deputy organizer of KOTM who drowned in Dora Lake on Halloween Eve in 1907. Herbert was one of many men who lost their lives working outdoors in the early days of the Northwoods.

The Lost 40 Scientific and Natural Area is an outdoor classroom for students of all ages. If you meet a group on the trail, pay close attention to the plants they study. Nature hikes and classes are held periodically during the summer months.

The Lost 40 Scientific and Natural Area, Forest Rd. 2240, Northome
dnr.state.mn.us

# VISIT
## WATERMARK ART CENTER

The Watermark Art Center captures Northwoods culture from an artist's eye. Past exhibits of note for culture and history seekers are the work of master bead artist Thomas Stillday, blankets by Rick Kagigebi, and the *Bring Her Home: Stolen Daughters of Turtle Island*. Exhibits change often, so visit several times a year.

The Watermark Art Center's name and location have changed several times through the years. Founded in 1982 when the Bemidji Community Art Center and Bemidji Art Center Association merged, the Watermark was originally called the Bemidji Community Arts Center (BCAC). At that time, it was housed in the Bemidji Carnegie Library which was built in 1909. BCAC moved across the street in 2012 and was renamed the Watermark Art Center in 2014. It's current location was secured in 2017.

Watermark Art Center, 505 Bemidji Ave. N, Bemidji
(218) 444-7570, watermarkartcenter.org

---

### TIP
Designed by W. D. Gillespie, and placed on the National Register of Historic Places in 1980, the treasured Carnegie Library underwent major renovations in 2019. It sits on the shores of beautiful Lake Bemidji, a perfect location for a picnic lunch after visiting the Watermark Art Center.

# WORK THE SOO LOCKS
## AT THE GREAT LAKES AQUARIUM

Starting to rain on your day in Duluth? A wet, cold day here is no problem if you stop at the Great Lakes Aquarium. The aquarium staff is constantly updating displays and adding new features. (I love the beavers!) All of the exhibits and activities at the Great Lakes Aquarium focus on the geological, natural, and cultural history of the Lake Superior area.

The giant fossils and live animals are cool to view. My all-time favorite activity is taking toy boats and navigating them through a large replica of the Soo Locks. I always get wet, and it takes me numerous times to remember the intricate details of the locks. It's much harder than it looks, and aquarium visitors gain a better understanding of the locks system.

Great Lakes Aquarium, 353 Harbor Dr., Duluth
(218) 740-3474

### TIP
The Great Lakes Aquarium prides itself in offering educational opportunities for children of all ages and all abilities. Please visit their website for specific programs and events for children with sensory sensitivities.

# STROLL THE BOARDWALK
## AT CROW WING STATE PARK

It's easy to picture yourself in the 1850s when you stroll through Crow Wing State Park. The historic boardwalk features interpretive signs that enable visitors to picture themselves in Crow Wing Village. Once a bustling community, Crow Wing Village met its demise in the 1870s due to a railroad crossing that was built in Brainerd.

Two cemeteries, the boardwalk, Red River Oxcart Trail, and the site of the 1768 Battle of Crow Wing are just a few of the historic sites to visit. The Catholic mission is well marked and contains headstones for many of the inhabitants. Friends of Old Crow Wing offer occasional demonstrations and programs. Take a walk on the boardwalk, and picture yourself in the mid-1800s.

Crow Wing State Park, 3124 State Park Rd., Brainerd
(218) 825-3075

# VISIT
## THE MOOSE LAKE DEPOT
## AND FIRES OF 1918 MUSEUM

Minnesota's worst natural disaster occurred in October 1918 and changed the landscape of the Minnesota Northwoods. Thirty-eight towns and villages burned; 453 people lost their lives, mostly between Moose Lake and Cloquet. Survivor recollections, artifacts, and memorabilia are on display at the Moose Lake Depot and Fires of 1918 Museum. The story of the Soderberg farm is recorded, in all its horror. Fourteen people hid in the family's root cellar as the fire approached, and all suffocated as the fire sucked every ounce of air from the structure.

After touring the Fires of 1918 Museum, visit the depot next door—the restored ticket counter and other original pieces of the railroad station are on display. A few miles away, in the Riverside Cemetery, stands a towering 27-foot monument where 200 fire victims are buried in a mass grave. It is a somber reminder of the fires.

The Moose Lake Depot and Fires of 1918 Museum
900 Folz Blvd., Moose Lake
(218) 485-4234, mooselakeareahistory.com

# SEE
## THE HILL MUSEUM & MANUSCRIPT LIBRARY

The Saint John's Bible in the Hill Museum & Manuscript Library was commissioned by the Benedictine Abbey in the late 1990s. It is the first such work appointed since the printing press was invented in the mid-1400s. The Saint John's Bible was completed in 2013, and has been on exhibit at various museums across the world.

This magnificent work of art is handwritten and hand illustrated, just like the bibles of early centuries. Master calligrapher Donald Jackson created the Saint John's Bible in 13 years. His tools, materials, and 28 original folios are also housed in the Saint John's Bible Gallery, along with rare books and manuscripts. This historical masterpiece is a must-see at least once in a person's lifetime.

Hill Museum and Manuscript Library, 2835 Abbey Plaza, Collegeville
(320) 363-3514, saintjohnsbible.org

# TIP

After looking at the Saint John's Bible, walk the campus and then drive six miles to the College of Saint Benedict. Tucked away in a tree-lined cemetery, hundreds of sisters have been laid to rest. Their cross markers are perfectly aligned and create a visual sense of awe.

# CLIMB ON TRUCKS
## AT THE MINNESOTA MUSEUM OF MINING

Iron ore mining was a major economic boom to the Minnesota Northwoods for many decades. The Minnesota Museum of Mining in Chisholm preserves and shares the history of mining on the Northwoods Iron Range. See a replica of an underground mine, climb on trucks with tires taller than an adult, check out the locomotive, and learn the history of mining. Once a logging town, Chisholm at its peak had 100 open-pit mines in operation. The mines are closed, but the history remains. Wear your old jeans so you can really get into the action.

The Minnesota Mining Museum is open Memorial Day through Labor Day. Educational and historic, a visit to the museum supplies students with great information for a summer research paper. Snap some fun photos and grab a piece of iron ore and their "What I Did This Summer" report will rock.

Minnesota Museum of Mining, 701 W Lake St., Chisholm
(218) 254-5543, mnmuseumofmining.org

# TAKE A RIDE
## ON THE NORTH SHORE SCENIC RAILROAD

The golden age of train travel has passed; however, you can experience some of its magic by taking a first-class ride on the *Duluth Zephyr*. The Silver Club Dome Car will woo you with a clear view of Lake Superior and deluxe seats. Narrators explain important landmarks from Duluth's past while you enjoy a cold beverage. The *Zephyr* also offers elegant dinner and murder mystery events to add to the charm of railroad travel.

Trains operate between Duluth and Two Harbors from May until December. Take a ride every season and watch the scenery change. The *clink, clink, clink* of the track will bring a smile to your face and nostalgia to your day.

North Shore Scenic Railroad, 506 W Michigan St., Duluth
(218) 722-1273, duluthtrains.com

### TIP
If your children are getting tired of walking, a train ride might be just the ticket! The whole family can view the Duluth lakeshore, without adding additional steps to a busy day.

Agates from Lake Superior's North Shore
Photo courtesy of Vicki Foss

# SHOPPING AND FASHION

# WARM YOUR TOES
## WITH STEGER MUKLUKS
## & MOCCASINS

A familiar phrase in these parts is that the Minnesota Northwoods has two seasons: winter and road construction, both lasting about six months. So, excellent winter footwear is a necessity, both for survival and outdoor enjoyment. The warmest winter boots in the world are made in Ely at Steger Mukluks & Moccasins. Will Steger wore a pair of Arctic Mukluks on his Artic expeditions, his feet stayed warm and dry. People as far away as Norway agree with Will that these boots are the best.

I love my Steger Mukluks. They're stylish and perfect for all-day wear. The Steger retail store also sells Chaco sandals, comfortable and stylish clothing, books, accessories, and Icelandic wool jackets (another necessity up north). The staff at Steger are friendly and patient. They'll help you find the perfect pair of mukluks for your winter activity.

Steger Mukluks and Moccasins, 33 E. Sheridan St., Ely
(218) 365-6634, mukluks.com

# FIND VARIETY
## AT CHRISTMAS POINT

Christmas Point is a shopping destination for the entire family. According to owners Scott and Jody Goehring, they are the Lakes Area source for home décor, unique gifts, clothing, a delicious café, and more. Although Christmas Point carries awesome Christmas items (think holly, jolly, over the top), their name comes from the road the family lived on for many years near Walker.

Two convenient locations (Walker and Baxter) make it easy to find just what you're looking for when traveling the Minnesota Northwoods. The Baxter store's three floors of goods offer a large selection of unique books, Northwoods clothing, housewares, wild rice, and wall art. Selecting the perfect gift for a family member or friend is easy. When you're done shopping, refuel with a chicken salad sandwich or panini with a side of fudge and specialty coffee.

14803 Edgewater Dr., Baxter          523 Minnesota Ave., Walker
(218) 828-0603                        (218) 547-2170
christmaspoint.com

# INDULGE IN LUXURY
## AT SERENITY NOW YARN & ALPACA SHOP

Natural alpaca fiber socks are so soft, warm, and snuggly. They make your feet happy and are perfect for our five long months of winter. Alpaca yarn makes great blankets and rugs, too. If you're in the mood to browse for socks, yarn, goat milk soap, and local artisanal goods, Serenity Now Yarn & Alpaca Shop is waiting for you. Small-town hospitality and big-city selection will meet you at the front door. The shop is locally owned and operated by Dave and Esther Endicott.

The Endicotts live on Esther's family's farm just a few miles from the shop. They give tours of the farm, including alpaca barns, livestock, and guardian dogs. Kids will get a kick out of seeing firsthand where alpaca fleece comes from. And adults will enjoy the fresh air.

Serenity Now Yarn and Alpaca Shop, 231 Barclay Ave., Pine River
(218) 587-1107, serenitynowalpacas.com

## TIP

I always get hungry after fresh air and shopping. Stop by Bites (#10) for a piece of cheesecake to hold you 'til dinner.

# GO NORTH
## TO RYDEN'S BORDER STORE

Ryden's Border Store is a half mile from the US/Canada border on Highway 61 (#61). I always stop on my trips into Canada for last-minute beverages and snacks, or anything I forgot to pack (like water shoes and sunscreen). On my way home, I stock up on any souvenirs I couldn't find in Thunder Bay. The selection is great, and prices are reasonable. Last year, my big find was Santa Fe Trail Route 66 beef jerky. It's 100 percent delicious and made in the USA—and takes the hangry out of long road trips.

A word of advice from a seasoned Ryden's Border Store shopper: Don't panic. Your cellphone is not broken. There is no cellphone service at the store, but they do have Wi-Fi you can connect to if needed. Now, go north or go south. The choice is yours.

Ryden's Border Store, 9301 Ryden Rd., Grand Portage
(218) 475-2330, rydensborderstore.com

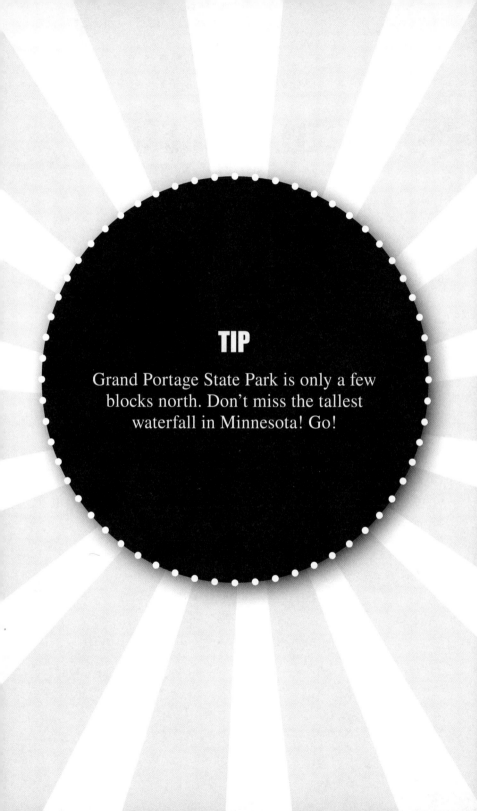

# TIP

Grand Portage State Park is only a few blocks north. Don't miss the tallest waterfall in Minnesota! Go!

# DAZZLE YOURSELF
## AT E.L. MENK JEWELERS

Ed Menk is a graduate gemologist. That's a fancy way of saying he knows his diamonds, and sapphires, and emeralds, and all the other gemstones that dazzle us. He tried to dazzle his wife for their anniversary in 1979 and bought the store his jewelry business resides in. She's never forgiven him, but patrons are grateful. (Ed has a great sense of humor.)

E.L. Menk is a full-service jewelry store that specializes in one-of-a-kind settings using new loose stones or your own heirloom stones. So, take that broken ruby ring out of your treasure chest, and have Ed and his staff create something you'll actually wear.

I encourage you to stop by the display of Ed's opal collection. He hand-cuts many of the stones in his workshop before creating unique necklaces, rings, and earrings. It's like Santa's workshop for adults.

E.L. Menk Jewelers, 623 Laurel St., Brainerd
(218) 829-7266, elmenkjewelers.com

# FIND WARMTH
## AT BEMIDJI WOOLEN MILLS

First winter in the Minnesota Northwoods? Stop at the Bemidji Woolen Mills for the warmth of natural wool to snuggle into. For 100 years, the Batchelder family has produced high-quality woolen outerwear as well as woolen underwear. From head to toe, inside and out, they have it all. The great benefit of buying quality apparel like this is that it doesn't go out of style. (Think buffalo plaid jackets.) Year after year, you'll stay warm, dry, and fashionable.

Bemidji Woolen Mills blankets and throws are a great gift for students heading off to college or newlyweds moving into their first home. Timeless patterns such as the Chief Joseph blanket (designed in 1920) are always the center of attention in rustic cabins and vacation homes.

Bemidji Woolen Mills, 301 Irvine Ave. NW, Bemidji
(218) 751-5166, bemidjiwoolenmills.com

# BROWSE FASHION AND MORE
## AT THE OLDE OPEN WINDOW

I'll share a few secrets I learned at the Olde Open Window. Boutique clothing doesn't have to drain your bank account. Business casual can be comfortable and stylish. And, no outfit is complete without a few strands of cat hair. Ask Benny, the cat.

Hardworking store cats meander through the merchandise, which is a mix of new, old, and handmade items. In addition to clothing, the Olde Open Window sells décor, souvenirs, accessories, antiques, and much more. Three floors of shopping await you.

The Olde Open Window, 602 Laurel St., Brainerd
(218) 454-3338

### TIP
The upper floor is home to a variety of old favorites and cool antiques such as lace baptismal gowns and "At the Lake" signs. New merchandise arrives every week, so meander through both floors when visiting the Olde Open Window.

# LOSE YOURSELF SHOPPING
## IN NISSWA

Lose yourself in Nisswa, where an abundance of small-town charm greets you at every shop entrance. One of the friendliest and most useful stores in Nisswa for travelers is Turtle Town Books & Gifts on Main Street. A new book, puzzle, game, or toy is a great way to start a family tradition when traveling through the Northwoods. On rainy afternoons, kids can challenge parents to a classic game of checkers, Yahtzee, or Apples to Apples. Or, pull out the Playmobile set, so you can finish your newest read.

Zaisers Gift Shop is another fun store to shop at. It has everything from aprons to zoo animals, all behind the hard-to-miss red door. They have a great selection of kitchen gadgets and table linens to spruce up your dining area. Speaking of spruce, they offer nature-themed gifts that will remind you of the Northwoods long after you leave. Dozens of other shops line the streets of Nisswa.

Nisswa Shopping
business.nisswa.com

# BUY AN AGATE
## AT AGATE CITY

As I mentioned in entry #49, Lake Superior agates (LSA) are Minnesota's state gemstone. A favorite activity in the Minnesota Northwoods is hunting for the elusive agate along the shores of Lake Superior. Agate City sells books that can point you in the right direction and help you locate your first LSA. If you leave the beach emptyhanded, don't fret. Agate City has thousands of agates on their shelves. One is sure to catch your eye.

But, don't be surprised if one of their other gifts or collectibles also calls out your name. If the sun shines just right, the store becomes a kaleidoscope of color. A colorful agate makes a unique gift for teachers, grandparents, and nature lovers of all ages. Rock polishers are a fun family project that will last for years.

Agate City, 721 7th Ave., Two Harbors
(218) 834-2304, agatecity.com

# TIP

When agate hunting, wear a hat
instead of sunglasses. Sunglasses
make it harder to see the waxy surface
and translucent glow of agates.

# SHOP BOOKS AND MORE
## AT CATTALE'S BOOKS & GIFTS

Prolific readers will have no trouble finding their next book at CatTale's Books & Gifts. The shelves are well-stocked with over 100,000 new, previously used, and rare books, including popular new-age titles. Spiritual gifts, rock specimens, aroma therapy, incense, gift cards, Fair Trade mittens, scarves, and comfortable reading ware are just a few of the many items at CatTale's. It's the type of store you enter with the intention of browsing and leave with a bag full of treasures.

CatTale's Books & Gifts, 609 Laurel St., Brainerd
(218) 825-8611, cattalesbooks.com

---

**TIP**
CatTales often hosts authors' book signings, especially for local authors new releases. Visit the store's website for event dates and times.

# BUY INDIGENOUS ART
## AT THE MILLE LACS INDIAN MUSEUM AND TRADING POST

The Mille Lacs Indian Museum and Trading Post's rich history dates back to 1918. The pristine log building has been beautifully restored to its 1930s charm. The history of this site is important, but equally so is the continuation of cultural heritage to sustain and encourage local artists to continue creating traditional art.

Renowned artists from tribes across North America proudly offer sculptures, paintings, jewelry, beadwork, baskets, moccasins, and much more. Over 250 contributors make the trading post the region's largest seller of Native American artwork. From the smallest leather bags to full-size wood sculptures, each item is beautifully crafted.

The trading post is part of the Minnesota Historical Society Mille Lacs site. Demonstrations and artist visits are located on the website. Minnesota Historical Society members save 10 percent on their purchases.

Mille Lacs Indian Museum and Trading Post
43411 Oodena Dr., Onamia
(320) 532-3632, mnhs.org

# GET OUTFITTED
## AT PIRAGIS NORTHWOODS COMPANY

The Boundary Waters Canoe Area (#44) is like the Wild West of Minnesota. Seriously, your cellphone won't work if you travel deep into it. It makes sense to visit a professional before venturing into the BWCA. Piragis Northwoods Company offers new gear, or you can rent what you need. It's your one-stop shop for a BWCA permit, maps, durable clothing, gear, books, and camp food that actually tastes good.

Try sitting on a camp chair that folds smaller than your favorite wine bottle. They weigh only a few pounds, so you can take them to the kids' soccer games and watch in comfort. Piragis canoe pants are another Northwoods favorite because they dry quickly without becoming stiff. Whether this is your first, or fiftieth trip to the BWCA, Piragis Northwoods Company has the supplies you need for a great adventure!

Piragis Northwoods Company, 105 N Central Ave., Ely
(218) 365-6745, piragis.com

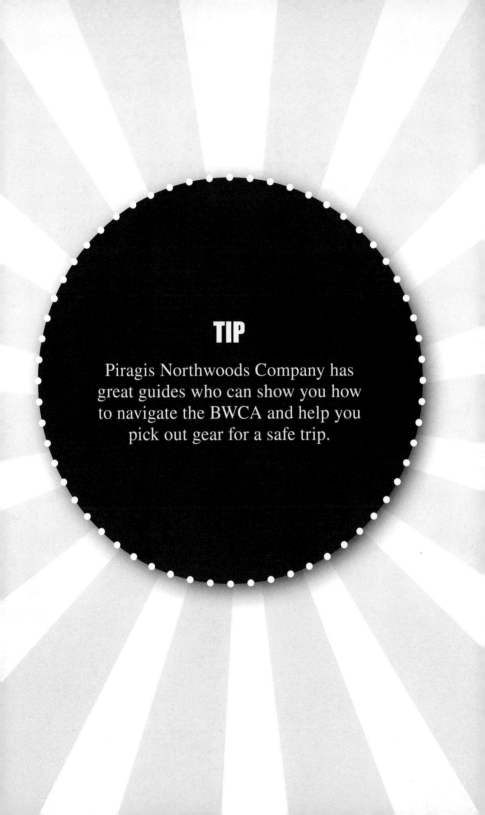

# TIP

Piragis Northwoods Company has great guides who can show you how to navigate the BWCA and help you pick out gear for a safe trip.

# EXCEED
# YOUR EXPECTATIONS
## AT DESIGN CONSIGN

Many consignment stores leave shoppers feeling underwhelmed and underserved, but not Design Consign. Just one look at the outside of this historic 1876 First National Bank building, and you'll see quality and selection. (You can also see the bullet holes from the 1933 bank robbery.) Inside, the large gallery-style showroom is tastefully set up with fine furniture, antiques, home décor, and really neat novelty items. Their holiday display puts everyone in the Christmas spirit.

Design Consign is a subsidiary company of S. Thomas & Associate Estate Sales. Many of the unique items in the store are from area estate sales. The selection changes every week, so stop by Design Consign whenever you're in the Brainerd Lakes area.

Design Consign, 201 S 6th St., Brainerd
(218) 824-0712, designconsignmn.com

# SHOP 'TIL YOU DROP
## AT FITGER'S SHOPPING MALL

Put on your walking shoes and get ready to power shop at the most unique shopping mall in Northwoods. Fitger's Brewhouse Brewery and Grille (#12) are only part of the picture. Your day begins with a morning cup of joe at Vanilla Bean Coffee House, followed by a historic walking tour through the complex. Floor by floor, the layout of the original brewery is revealed. From the taproom to the boiler room, and on to the engine house, it's all there for you to see.

After the self-guided tour, the Duluth Kitchen Co., The Bookstore at Fitger's (Duluth's only independent bookstore), Fitger's Wine Cellar, Lotus on the Lake, and Trailfitters will be easy to find. With almost two dozen shops and restaurants, I encourage you to book a room at Fitger's Hotel so you can drop off your shopping bags between floors!

Fitger's Shopping Mall
fitgers.com/fitgers-shopping-mall

# WANDER
## THROUGH WALKER

Finding Lucette (#73) won't take long (she is 17 feet tall, after all), so you'll have lots of time to wander through downtown Walker. Park on the 400 block of Minnesota Avenue West, where you can stroll and shop for blocks.

The first stop is the Walker General Store for a great Minnesota Northwoods souvenir sweatshirt or mug. They have a sizeable selection of toys, puzzles, and games for the children.

The next stop is Lundrigans Clothing for quality sportswear, coats, shoes, and boots for the whole family. I really enjoy their lightweight summer shirts while I'm boating. Prices are a little higher than at the big-box stores, but the quality and selection are excellent.

Loide Oils & Vinegars have healthy balsamic vinegars and food items you crave for freshness. I suggest you try the black cherry balsamic vinegar on seasonal summer salads.

You'll find a second Christmas Point (#87) a few doors down. The store is smaller than their Baxter location, but has a great selection! Keep wandering for more Minnesota Northwoods shopping.

**Walker General Store**
420 Minnesota Ave. W, Walker
(218) 547-0686

**Lundrigans Clothing**
501 Minnesota Ave. W, Walker
(218) 547-1041

**Loide Oils & Vinegars**
513 Minnesota Ave. W, Walker
(218) 547-6457

E.L. Menk Jeweler
Photo courtesy of Vicki Foss

# SUGGESTED
## ITINERARIES

## ADULT BEVERAGE TOURS

Relax at Cuyuna Brewing Company, 22

Enjoy a Ms. Galena at the Roundhouse Brewery, 4

Choose a Minnesota Northwoods Wine, 12

Enjoy the View at Moose Lake Brewery, 7

Try Poutine with Your Beer at Fitger's Brewhouse Brewery and Grille, 16

## DATE NIGHT

Ride in a Horse-Drawn Carriage by Duluth's Waterfront, 39

Dazzle Yourself at E.L. Menk Jewelers, 116

Catch Live Music at Wussow's Concert Café, 51

Find Treasures on a Glensheen Mansion Tour, 86

Enjoy the View at Moose Lake Brewery, 7

Tour the Lights at Bentleyville, 48

Walk Up to the High Falls at Grand Portage State Park, 71

## FUN WITH KIDS

Be Amazed by the Ski Loons Water Ski Show, 78

Find Variety at Christmas Point, 111

Work the Soo Locks at the Great Lakes Aquarium, 101

Buy Indigenous Art at the Mille Lacs Indian Museum and Trading Post, 123

Catch Legendary Walleyes on Mille Lacs Lake, 82

• • • • • • • • • • • • • • • • • • • • • • • • • • •

## EERIE STOPS

## ANIMAL LOVERS

## RAINY DAYS

• • • • • • • • • • • • • • • • • • • • • • • • • • •

## SCENIC HIGHWAY 61

## RACK UP SOME STEPS

• • • • • • • • • • • • • • • • • • • • • • • •

Bearing it in the Northwoods
Photo courtesy of Sebastian Paczuski

# ACTIVITIES
## BY SEASON

## WINTER

Try Jams and Jellies at Butkiewicz Family Farm, 6

Start Your Holidays at the Christmas City of the North Parade, 30

Watch the John Beargrease Sled Dog Marathon, 65

Bring in the Holidays with Concordia College's Holiday Concert, 38

Tour the Lights at Bentleyville, 48

Win a Truck at the Jaycees Ice Fishing Extravaganza, 60

Feel the Breeze as You Downhill Ski, 72

## SPRING

Watch Hawks at Hawk Ridge Bird Observatory, 58

Count Birds at the Annual Sax Zim Bog Birding Festival, 67

## SUMMER

White Water Raft with Swiftwater Adventures, 83

Find Your Groove at the Bayfront Blues Festival, 32

See Bears Up Close at the Vince Shute Wildlife Sanctuary, 62

Be Amazed by the Ski Loons Water Ski Show, 78

Dance at Iskigamizigan Powwow, 44

• • • • • • • • • • • • • • • • • • • • • • • • •

# FALL

Milford Mine Memorial Park
Photo courtesy of Vicki Foss

# INDEX

• • • • • • • • • • • • • • • • • • • • • • • • • • • •

• • • • • • • • • • • • • • • • • • • • • • • • • •

● ● ● ● ● ● ● ● ● ● ● ● ● ● ● ● ● ● ● ● ● ● ● ● ●

Fancy Pants Chocolates
Photo courtesy of Vicki Foss